"Is God doing a new thing? I dare to say that he is! And the reader into a renewed wonder and enchantment of a God who is moving toward creation and inviting it into the intimate love of God. This book made me want to be a missionary again. Not somewhere else, but right here."

A.J. Swoboda, associate professor of Bible and theology at Bushnell University and author of *The Gift of Thorns*

"This book is a well-written exploration of contemporary mission in culturally diverse, post-Christian contexts. It is not just a good example of robust but accessible theological reflection, it is also grounded in the living experience of the authors. Good stuff!"

Alan Hirsch, author of *The Forgotten Ways* and founder of Forge Missional Training Network and the Movement Leaders Collective

"While some missional literature sounds grave warnings about the parlous state of the church today, *Reviving Mission* is rooted in an infectious optimism about the unfurling of the kingdom and the church's role in it. The authors believe God is up to something, and their book is a clarion call for us to take our place in the new season he is stirring up around the world. Inspiring and practical."

Michael Frost, founder of the Tinsley Institute at Morling College in Sydney, Australia, and coauthor with Christiana Rice of *To Alter Your World*

"If you want to turn from cynicism to wonder, read this book! Linson Daniel, Jon Hietbrink, and Eric Rafferty testify to how God is at work in our world through those who seek him. Understanding the 4*E* framework illustrated in *Reviving Mission* transfers mission from professionals to everyday Christ-followers. This is a *kairos* moment: as we look toward God's future, anticipating it in the present, we can participate with the God of history in creating a future filled with unshakable joy!"

JR Woodward, national director of the V3 Movement and author of *Creating a Missional Culture*

"God is on the move and doing a new thing in our fast-changing world. *Reviving Mission* is full of practical insights and thoughtful reflections from seasoned Christian leaders that apply to all who want to understand God's work for our times and wrestle with the challenges of living out their faith. A must-read for all serious Christians everywhere."

Sam George, global catalyst for diasporas with the Lausanne Movement and author of *Sharing Jesus with Hindus*

"The missional frame of this book—encounter, explore, empower, establish—is so helpful in starting and sustaining flourishing communities of faith. This is the way to do it! And the stories the authors share offer much inspiration and hope that God is still on the move today. If you want practical ways to jump in and be a part of what God is doing in the world, read this book."

James Choung, vice president of strategy and innovation of InterVarsity Christian Fellowship/USA, and coauthor with Ryan Pfeiffer of *Longing for Revival*

"A must-read primer for any ministry leader hoping to be better equipped and empowered. *Reviving Mission* offers much-needed postures and practical tools that will not only revive your mission but also your faith. God is doing something new!"

Tom Lin, president and CEO of InterVarsity Christian Fellowship/USA

"*Reviving Mission* is a fresh, innovative integration of spiritual formation and holistic missiology pointing us to something bigger that's going on all around us—a fresh move of God in our time! Drawing us into practical rhythms that invite us to encounter God, *Reviving Mission* seeks to normalize a movement posture. Demonstrating that God can and does move in power anywhere and everywhere, the authors call us to a fresh hope for revival and awakening at this cultural moment. This is a must-read for anyone passionate about cultural transformation, movement, and revival."

R. York Moore, CEO of the Coalition for Christian Outreach

"Guiding us beyond immature triumphalism and reactive disillusionment, Linson Daniel, Jon Hietbrink, and Eric Rafferty give us a renewed vision for mission with their wise and practical book. Yes, as they argue, mission must be revived, avoiding the political distortions and cultural mistakes of the past, made alive for everyday life with the real presence of Jesus! Their holistic vision is both good news for communities that we are sent to and for all those who are sent. A wonderful and much-needed resource!"

Daniel D. Lee, academic dean of the Asian American Center at Fuller Theological Seminary and author of *Doing Asian American Theology*

"This book is for those who hunger for renewal and long to see God's renewing work spill out beyond the walls of the church. Combining hope-driven inspiration and practical solutions, *Reviving Mission* is a wonderful resource that will equip and encourage the priesthood of all believers for our God-given mission in the world."

Mark Sayers, senior pastor of Red Church in Melbourne, Australia, and author of *Reappearing Church*

"Faith-building, discerning, and robust! New seasons require new wineskins. *Reviving Mission* provides a fresh expression of new wineskins that can steward a move of God in our generation."

Sarah Breuel, Revive Europe executive director and Lausanne Movement board member

"In *Reviving Mission*, Linson Daniel, Jon Hietbrink, and Eric Rafferty so poignantly call the church—young and old alike—to join the mission of God in reviving us to the presence and movement of God in our lives so we can help revive the people and places around us. This is a primer on how to participate in everyday missions while preparing for generational revival. If you desire to experience more of God's presence in your life, discover how God is currently moving around you, and empower others to be multiplying witnesses of Jesus, this book is a must-read!"

Thai Lam, executive director of the Revival Is Family Foundation and director of the Collegiate Day of Prayer

"In *Reviving Mission*, authors Linson Daniel, Jon Hietbrink, and Eric Rafferty take readers back to the fundamentals, when authentic encounters with Jesus provided purpose and direction for the lives of his followers. The authors remind us that God's presence, and not political motivations, renowned success, or extravagant church services, is what is needed to bring true transformation. God is moving, and this book shows us how to follow him into a new season where he will bring life to people across the globe."

Dave Ferguson, author of *Hero Maker* and *B.L.E.S.S.*

"Throughout all of history, we have seen fresh moves of the Spirit. Some become historical moments noted in the media, while others are personal but no less world changing. *Reviving Mission* looks at some practical steps in how to be a Holy Spirit people in the places where God leads us, and I am grateful for a book that so accessibly equips those who want to see the kingdom come on earth as it is in heaven."

Jay Pathak, national director of Vineyard USA

"Linson Daniel, Jon Hietbrink, and Eric Rafferty's significant contribution to mission in the twenty-first century isn't what we would expect. While loaded with large canvases of theological and biblical acumen, *Reviving Mission* doesn't just stop there: it provides story after story of the real lives of real people who have made real decisions around practicing reviving mission through their real encounters and exploration with God, resulting in the real empowerment of leaders and establishing real communities of Jesus."

Eun K. Strawser, author of *Centering Discipleship* and president of Iwa Collaborative

"A powerful invitation for ordinary people to join God's extraordinary movement, embodying his reviving mission in our chaotic world. With rich mission theology and evidence of God's fresh work in new expressions of global revival, *Reviving Mission* offers a hopeful, practical blueprint for living out our faith with renewed purpose and passion. Linson Daniel, Jon Hietbrink, and Eric Rafferty are sure to inspire, challenge, and equip younger generations to bring God's kingdom to life in every aspect of daily life, starting with personal encounters with God and extending to empowering others as missional disciples."

Beth Seversen, former associate pastor of youth and Christian ministries studies at North Park University, author of *Not Done Yet: Reaching and Keeping Unchurched Emerging Adults*

REVIVING MISSION

AWAKENING TO THE EVERYDAY MOVEMENT OF GOD

LINSON DANIEL, JON HIETBRINK,
AND ERIC RAFFERTY

An imprint of InterVarsity Press
Downers Grove, Illinois

InterVarsity Press
P.O. Box 1400 | Downers Grove, IL 60515-1426
ivpress.com | email@ivpress.com

©2024 by Linson Thomas Daniel, Jonathan Paul Hietbrink, Eric Rafferty, and InterVarsity Christian Fellowship/USA

All rights reserved. No part of this book may be reproduced in any form without written permission from InterVarsity Press.

InterVarsity Press® is the publishing division of InterVarsity Christian Fellowship/USA®. For more information, visit intervarsity.org.

All Scripture quotations, unless otherwise indicated, are taken from The Holy Bible, New International Version®, NIV®. Copyright © 1973, 1978, 1984, 2011 by Biblica, Inc.™ Used by permission of Zondervan. All rights reserved worldwide. www.zondervan.com. The "NIV" and "New International Version" are trademarks registered in the United States Patent and Trademark Office by Biblica, Inc.™

While any stories in this book are true, some names and identifying information may have been changed to protect the privacy of individuals.

The publisher cannot verify the accuracy or functionality of website URLs used in this book beyond the date of publication.

Cover design: David Fassett
Interior design: Jeanna Wiggins
Images: iStock / Getty Images Plus: ©Valery Rybakou, © Burhan Adiatma

ISBN 978-1-5140-0962-8 (print) | ISBN 978-1-5140-0963-5 (digital)

Printed in the United States of America ♾

Library of Congress Cataloging-in-Publication Data
A catalog record for this book is available from the Library of Congress.

31 30 29 28 27 26 25 24 | 12 11 10 9 8 7 6 5 4 3 2 1

To

Sophia, JT,

Elijah, Abigail,

Memo, Elena, Jonny,

and all future heralds

OF THE

reviving mission of Jesus

CONTENTS

Preface: Signs of a New Season   1

1   A New Season and a New Way   5

2   Jesus' Holistic Mission   26

3   Encounter: *God Is Here*   44

4   Encounter: *God Is Moving*   63

5   Explore: *Lift Up Your Eyes*   80

6   Explore: *People of Peace*   98

7   Empower: *By What Power?*   119

8   Empower: *Serve and Send*   139

9   Establish: *God of Cadence*   158

10   Establish: *God of the Garden-City*   176

Conclusion: The Joy of Jesus   199

Epilogue: Heralds of a New Normal   211

Acknowledgments   215

Notes   219

Preface

SIGNS OF A NEW SEASON

SOMETHING CURIOUS HAPPENED in the countryside of Kentucky in the spring of 2023. What started as an everyday chapel service on the campus of Asbury University—a few familiar songs, an ordinary sermon, and the typical crowd of sincere but drowsy college students—became something very different when the gospel choir tasked to end the service decided not to close but to continue in worship.

Before long, reports started to circulate on campus about "something happening" in Hughes Auditorium, and students began to return in droves to worship, pray, and pour out their hearts in confession. Momentum continued to build through the evening as hundreds of students filled the chapel, lingering together in the presence of God.

That same day, a campus minister at the University of Kentucky had his phone turned off for a retreat day. When he flipped it back on that night, he was taken aback as hundreds of text messages about "something happening at Asbury" arrived simultaneously. When he drove to campus that night, he found the chapel packed with students and the altar at the front of the auditorium "wet with tears" of repentance.[1]

What had begun as a one-hour chapel service for a couple dozen Asbury students quickly became something of a spiritual phenomenon. Word began to spread about an "outpouring" on campus. Tens of thousands of students and adults from hundreds of campuses and dozens of countries—all of them pilgrims of one sort or another—began to descend on Wilmore, Kentucky, to experience for themselves what God was doing. Worship and prayer continued around the clock for more than two weeks, culminating on the two hundredth anniversary of the Collegiate Day of Prayer (CDOP). In what became a remarkable demonstration of divine symmetry, more than a year beforehand, CDOP had arranged to stream its annual simulcast of prayer for the campuses of America on the last Thursday of February from none other than Hughes Auditorium at Asbury University.

As my (Jon's) family followed what was happening at Asbury from a distance, we became increasingly eager to make our own pilgrimage to the campus to bear witness to what God was doing. In response to this growing conviction, we made plans to be on site for the CDOP simulcast on the evening of February 23.

After landing in Lexington, we started our drive through the rolling green countryside of Kentucky. As Midwesterners still mired in the throes of winter back home, our spirits were enlivened by the signs of spring so clearly emerging all around us: birds were singing, trees were budding, and daffodils were blooming.

We arrived that afternoon to gather and pray with some friends at a local church, and as we entered the auditorium a couple hours before the official service, we were struck by the juxtaposition between the profoundly ordinary setting of the chapel—concrete floors, wooden seats, an unadorned stage—and the extraordinary sense of God's presence hanging in the air.

Signs of a New Season

By any account, the scene was strikingly *analog*. In contrast to the hyperdigital, technology-saturated environments that we've grown accustomed to, the setting at Asbury was spartan and the aesthetic was simple. There were no thumping subwoofers, no intricate lighting schemes, no multimedia visual effects, and not a single screen in sight (not even for lyrics). It was an unadorned and uncomplicated backdrop: an analog space.

The environment was marked by an arresting *anonymity*. Despite the culminating service being live-streamed to tens of thousands of people around the world, the event continued with the pattern that had been established earlier in the outpouring—no one introduced themselves to the room. There was no mention of status or position. Indeed, no one even mentioned their own name. In that chapel the name of Jesus was the only one that mattered; everyone else was free to be delightfully anonymous.

The experience at Asbury was refreshingly *amateur*. Instead of professionals running the show, the experience was led by students who, while gifted and sincere, were also not world-class musicians or speakers. Worship flowed from consecration, even if it was slightly off-key. Testimonies centered on the simple reading of "life verse" Scriptures rather than eloquently polished expositions. Though the outpouring was supported by a group of humble and seasoned leaders, what was significant in that chapel was not the quality of one's credentials—the mark of a professional. It was the quality of one's affection—the mark of an amateur, an English word that has its root in the Latin *amare*, which means, quite simply, "to love."

Like the way that individual flowers emerge en masse from the soil each spring, the outpouring at Asbury was simultaneously personal and collective. The space was populated by countless individual encounters with God—each beautiful and profound—but taken together, those experiences testified to something much larger going on.

That evening my family was honored to worship and pray alongside hundreds of students in the auditorium and thousands more on campuses across the country who were participating via livestream. The experience left an enduringly personal mark on us. I will never forget sharing a time of intergenerational blessing with my son and watching my daughter offer her heart to God in worship. Simultaneously, we were keenly aware that we—just like those around us—were a part of a decidedly communal experience; something bigger was going on. Together with the community, we were bearing witness as God poured out his Spirit and a generation offered their collective "yes" to Jesus.

Sometimes extraordinary things happen, and it's easy to assume that those things are anomalies—unique, random, and isolated from any kind of broader narrative. They may be delightful, but they are aberrations destined for a footnote in the history books.

However, sometimes those extraordinary things aren't anomalies at all—they are heralds testifying to something just over the horizon, they are forerunners embodying an oncoming future, they are signs of a new season emerging all around us.

A NEW SEASON AND A NEW WAY

Forget the former things;
do not dwell on the past.
See, I am doing a new thing!
Now it springs up; do you not perceive it?
I am making a way in the wilderness
and streams in the wasteland.

Isaiah 43:18-19

We believe God is doing something new.

Just as the horizon begins to glow before the dawn and thunder from an oncoming storm rumbles before rain starts to fall, we believe we're seeing signs of a new season at hand.

While the outpouring at Asbury was certainly beautiful, what's remarkable is that it was not exceptional. During the spring of 2023, reports started to emerge from numerous campuses across the United States that God was moving in similar ways—pouring out fresh expressions of his love and encountering students with his presence.

In the weeks before and after the outpouring at Asbury, historically Black colleges and universities (HBCUs) like Jackson State reported movements of prayer that led to dozens of students surrendering their lives to Jesus in repentance. One campus minister at Tuskegee University wondered if she was in the wrong room when she showed up to her first Bible study of the year and found over a hundred students gathered together eager to encounter God!

Smaller Christian schools like Lee University, Cedarville University, and Azusa Pacific found their chapels full of students stirred to day-and-night worship and intercession saturated by the presence of God.[1]

Large public universities like Purdue, Auburn, Texas A&M, and Florida State hosted student gatherings that filled venues and overflowed into spontaneous public baptisms in campus ponds and public fountains previously used to haze students after nights of excessive partying.[2]

Student conferences began to sell out and become standing-room-only events. One such retreat in Utah had booked a hotel anticipating a gathering of several hundred students, but because of the overwhelming interest, had to set up a (revival?) tent in the parking lot to accommodate everyone who wanted to attend.

Across the country, testimonies from experienced campus ministers of all types began to resound with a common refrain—"We've never seen spiritual hunger like this." Together, they marveled as a generation of students whose lives were indelibly marked by the Covid-19 pandemic found themselves living the words of the prophet Joel, who promised that the Lord "will repay you for the years the locusts have eaten" (Joel 2:25).

Though historic in its own context, what God has been doing on campuses across the United States is but an echo of the dynamic ways God is moving all around the world. As Nana Yaw Offei Awuku, director of the Lausanne Younger Leaders Generation

A New Season and a New Way

initiative,[3] has said, "Though things may *look* stagnant, below the surface, something is *boiling*."[4]

In the spring of 2024, God moved in power at a conference in East London cohosted by a coalition of diverse ministries and three churches who had formerly seen each other as rivals. Hundreds of young people in attendance responded to a call to holiness—at one point the entire conference was lying prostrate before God—and consecrated themselves to the Lord through a spontaneous, all-night prayer vigil. Experienced leaders from around the world who attended the event testified to the unique sense of God's presence upon the gathering saying, "I've never seen anything like it."[5]

In France, a country known for its secularism, new expressions of faith are emerging. The National Council of French Evangelicals (CNEF) reports that, on average, one new church is being planted every week,[6] and more than twelve thousand people were baptized across the country on Easter Sunday 2024.[7]

Rather than allow their rhythms of prayer and worship to be disrupted by Covid-19 lockdowns, university students in Bergen, Norway, gathered to seek God every week of the pandemic by meeting *outside*, often in freezing temperatures and snow. What began as a collection of hungry students on a single campus has now become an international network of like-minded missional communities reaching to England, Germany, and Denmark.[8]

Countries in Latin America are seeing a surge in spiritual passion, and a region that was once primarily a mission-receiving field is now becoming a mission-sending force. Shortly before the pandemic, THE SEND Brazil convened 140,000 people in three different stadiums for a twelve-hour event focused on mobilizing young people for the Great Commission.[9]

Recently, stories have surfaced from around the globe (including Thailand,[10] Nigeria,[11] and Southern California[12]) of mass public baptism events where more than a thousand people have chosen to be baptized in a single instance—stories that echo back to the Jesus Movement of the 1970s.

As globalization has amplified, God has been using the migration of people to accelerate mission in surprising ways. Over the last thirty years, thousands of churches have been planted by Latin American immigrants[13] in countries like Spain and Portugal, and some African denominations now include over 750 congregations across England, where they are continuing to plant an average of twenty-five new churches a year![14] In a striking inversion of missiological history, many wonder whether God might be using these "diaspora churches" to help re-evangelize increasingly secular populations.[15]

Further, God is using house-church movements around the world like those in China to accelerate his mission on a global scale. The Lausanne Movement now estimates that "2,000 mainland Chinese house-church missionaries serve cross-culturally overseas,"[16] and globally, "there are now 9 million churches emerging from or part of a CPM (church-planting movement)"—an increase of 350 percent in the last ten years.[17]

Fueled by the dynamic movement of God in countries like Nigeria, Ethiopia, and Kenya, it's currently projected that 50 percent of the world's Christians will live in Africa by 2050, and even predominantly Muslim nations like Guinea-Bissau are seeing massive crowds flock to evangelistic events. After one such gathering, thousands of teenagers took to the streets in the capital city singing songs of worship and proclaiming the gospel.[18]

In Iran, where there were fewer than three hundred known believers in 1970, there are now reports that perhaps a million people have come to faith, a trend which would make the Iranian church the fastest-growing church in the world.[19] Though staggering to consider, it's believed that more Iranian Muslims have come to faith in Christ in the last fifty years than in the previous fourteen centuries combined.[20]

Though these stories—and *thousands* more like them that are emerging around the world—are sourced in radically different contexts, it's remarkable to consider what they have in common and how they paint a collective picture of the new thing God is doing in our day.

These are movements fueled not by flashy effects but faithful obedience. These stories are not monodirectional but polycentric and rooted in the collaborative partnership of the whole body of Christ. They aren't directed by leaders with vast social media networks but anonymous saints laying down their lives (sometimes literally) for the sake of Jesus. These are movements whose primary actors aren't paid professionals but ordinary people offering their sincere yes to God's invitation—amateurs compelled not by their credentials but their love. These are movements that, while exceptional in impact, are decidedly everyday in spirit.

It's been said that when it comes to reports of revival, one would "far rather be gullible than cynical," and this is a sentiment that resonates in our own spirits.[21] We've lived enough life and led enough ministry to know that things often don't work out as we'd planned, and to hope is to risk disappointment.

Even so, we find ourselves wondering at what God is doing in our day, and our conviction in writing this book is that these kinds of stories—whether spontaneous or coordinated—aren't isolated incidents.[22] Rather, just as trees bud in anticipation of spring, we believe they are signs of a new season that God is releasing. Our contention is that the everyday characteristics of these movements are in fact an invitation to us as God's people in this cultural moment. We believe he is calling the church to awaken to the everyday movement of God all around us—he's inviting us to embrace his reviving mission.

WINTER AND SPRING

Just as resurrection is only possible after death, spring only arrives after winter, and we can all agree that this has been a season of "winter" around the world.[23]

From global catastrophes like the Covid-19 pandemic and the climate crisis; to contempt-fueled conflicts in Ukraine, Israel, and Gaza; to escalating refugee crises around the world; to rising political polarization, the last few years have been uniquely marked by death and disruption.

Here in the United States, we are navigating multiple simultaneous sociopolitical crises that have only added to the disintegration so many of us feel.[24] Cultural issues like the amplification of Christian nationalism, tension caused by ongoing racial injustice, shifting cultural norms around human sexuality, and the mental health crisis have had a compounding effect on our communities. Many within and beyond the church feel increasingly disenfranchised by and cynical toward institutions once thought to be trustworthy.

Unfortunately, the American church has not been immune to these disruptions. Too often we have been complicit in propagating a kind of counterfeit Christianity marked by narcissistic leadership, the co-opting of biblical truth to suit a political agenda, and the reinforcement of systems that have fostered spiritual abuse. This kind of imitation faith has had a profound impact on the community of faith and the church's credibility in the broader culture.

Internally, many of us who still identify as Christians find ourselves increasingly dissatisfied with what feels like an anemic spirituality that pales in comparison to what we see in the New Testament. Further, many of us are disillusioned by the idolatry being exposed among God's people and resonate with those who are actively deconstructing their faith. It's hard not to be cynical about the future of the church when we've had to endure an endless exposé of toxic systems like those captured in *The Rise and Fall of Mars Hill*, *Shiny Happy People*, or the parade of scandals involving previously respected Christian leaders.[25]

Externally, the result has been an erosion of credibility for the church in the West—particularly among younger generations who are abandoning faith traditions at an alarming rate.[26] Fueled in part by a legitimate critique of the ways that historic "Christian mission" has often been co-opted by colonialism and used as an excuse for exploitation, many young people increasingly view "mission" as synonymous with oppression and Christianity as devoid of integrity. They see the ways we have been compromised by unholy alliances that render us at best irrelevant and, at worst, part of the problem to be resisted.

WHAT'S "OUT THERE" IS "IN HERE"

Of course, the issue is that we all know—at least in our honest moments—that the problem of counterfeit faith isn't just "out there" with others; it's also "in here"—latent in our own lives. Though perhaps not to the extent as the exploitative expressions above, the same issues that plague the collective life of God's people also shape our own stories.

We too know what it's like to live a life of feeble faith absent of transformational power. We know that our hearts are saturated with skepticism. We experience the same kind of pervasive weariness and fatigue that marks our culture.[27] We too know how it feels to experience contempt toward those different from us. We also know what it's like to be more concerned about our comfort than compelled by our convictions. We too are familiar with a reticence to risk that leaves us unwilling to relinquish control. We are often marked by the same ambient anxiety as the world around us.[28]

It's the throes of winter that make us yearn for spring. Despite the gaps we see "out there" and "in here," stories like those above testify to a fresh hunger that is beginning to stir. People everywhere—young and old alike—are longing to live lives marked by wonder, curiosity, generosity, and resilience. The world—though calloused by counterfeit Christianity—is as desperate as ever for a real, authentic experience of what is true. We, the people of God, are eager for a movement of God that might lead us into beautifully everyday expressions of reviving mission.

REVIVING MISSION

This book is rooted in a few core convictions. First, we know that the world and the church need revival. Due to the disruptions of these years and a chronic pattern of compromise, we have lost the way of Jesus. Second, we rejoice that God is doing something new in our day—we believe that we are entering a new season that will be marked by the everyday movement of God. Third, we are convinced that a new season calls for a new way forward—a fresh expression of holistic mission rooted in the life of Jesus that can steward the season we are entering.

We chose to name this book *Reviving Mission* because we love the ways this phrase resonates with these convictions.

First, *Reviving Mission* speaks to the ways *our conceptions of mission need to be revived*. Too often Christian mission has not resembled the way of Jesus, and our credibility has been compromised. However, rather than abandoning gospel mission altogether, we believe that our understanding and practice of mission need to be revived. We need a fresh articulation of authentic kingdom mission in our increasingly broken world.

Second, *Reviving Mission* speaks to the *impact of mission on the people and communities we are sent to*. Jesus' mission is a reviving mission that embodies resurrection life in places of death and expresses the kingdom of God "on earth as it is in heaven." Just like Ezekiel's prophetic vision of a river flowing from the temple—"where the river flows everything will live" (Ezekiel 47:9)—so too the mission of Jesus revives neighborhoods and workplaces, campuses and countries, cities and families. Jesus invites us to join him in this mission as agents of revival in a world that is thirsty for renewal.

Finally, *Reviving Mission* speaks to the *impact of mission on the people and communities who are sent*. Instead of a mission that burns people out to bring revival to others, the promise of mission in the way of Jesus is that it is reviving for us as missionaries. Jesus invites us to taste the resurrection life we testify about. Our conviction is that Jesus' reviving mission transforms not only the mission field but also the mission force and enables us to live lives of flourishing faith.

THE NEW WAY IS AN OLD WAY

There's a Ghanaian proverb based on the Sankofa bird that translates as, "It is wise to go back to the ways you have forgotten."[29] Often the only way we can move forward is to look back and bring the treasures of the past into the future.

Though we believe that a new season calls for a new way forward, our conviction is that this new way isn't something we need to create; it's something we need to rediscover. In fact, we're convinced that the new way is actually an old way.

Centuries of history and the apparatus of Christendom[30] can make us think Jesus was a kind of stained-glass superhero.[31] However, when we consider the sociopolitical backdrop of a first-century Mediterranean world ruled by emperors and elites, it's fitting to describe Jesus' life and the movement he started as decidedly "everyday."

We know virtually nothing of the first thirty years of Jesus' life beyond that he lived as a craftsman in a small Galilean village far from anything resembling the halls of power in Rome. He was conceived under socially dubious circumstances, fled his home as a refugee, lost his adopted father sometime during his upbringing, and was no stranger to family drama. Jesus was an everyday kind of guy.

The genesis of his ministry was a profound encounter with God as he was baptized in the Jordan River along with crowds of Jewish pilgrims. After a forty-day period of consecration in the wilderness, he launched his ministry not in Jerusalem, but a fishing village down the road from his hometown—a very everyday sort of place.

Even as he started preaching and performing decidedly extraordinary miracles, he was regularly found eating with friends (and no doubt some strangers) around a table of shared hospitality. Indeed, the families who welcomed him soon became spiritual families, and their everyday homes—whether those of Peter or Levi or Mary—soon became home bases from which he ministered.

As Jesus grew in friendship with a group of decidedly ordinary folks, he called them to become his disciples—that they might be with him and be sent out with authority as his representatives.[32] Despite their lack of formal leadership training, they accepted his invitation, and these ordinary people started to do what Jesus had done—extraordinary things like preaching about the kingdom of God, healing diseases, and delivering those around them from demonic affliction.

Over the coming years, this group of friends would traverse the countryside of Israel witnessing the remarkable but also wrestling with confusion and making a host of mistakes. Through it all Jesus taught them how to live a different kind of everyday life: how to pray, how to love, how to forgive, how to be grateful, and (we have to imagine) how to tell a good joke.[33]

Though it started under the radar, eventually this new kind of everyday life threatened the established powers, and Jesus met an everyday kind of death. He was executed as a common criminal, alone and abandoned by almost everyone, including (apparently) the God he had entrusted himself to. He was buried without fanfare in a stranger's tomb by people who barely knew him while his closest friends fled into hiding.

Of course, we now know that Jesus' death was anything but ordinary and on the third day something historically extraordinary happened as he was resurrected from the dead. In the remarkable days that followed, he once again took up his regular patterns of eating with his friends in homes and teaching his disciples how to embody this new, everyday way until he (shockingly!) left them in charge and told them to wait for the gift he'd promised to send them.

As the disciples continued to do what they had always done with Jesus—gathering together and spending time in earnest prayer—the gift Jesus had promised arrived in the person of the Holy Spirit. Energized by that gift, Jesus' followers began replicating his way everywhere they went. Though they were later described derisively as "unschooled, ordinary men" (Acts 4:13), Jesus' friends bore witness to his life first in Jerusalem and Judea, then in Samaria, and eventually to the very ends of the earth. Church history records that Jesus' disciples traveled as far as Turkey (Philip), Rome (Simon Peter), England (Simon the Zealot), Ethiopia (Matthew), and India (Thomas), and that each of them laid down their lives for their friend.[34]

Though it's hard to know how much true societal change they might have seen by the end of their lives,[35] in time they became a living embodiment of Jesus' parable of the yeast that worked through the whole batch of dough (Luke 13:20-21). In the space of just three hundred years, this ordinary group of friends, fueled by extraordinary affection for Jesus, had upended the Roman Empire and altered the course of global history.[36]

For all the ways Christians have failed to embody the image of Jesus, his everyday followers had an undeniable impact on ancient society, as secular sociologist Rodney Stark reflects in his seminal work *The Rise of Christianity*:

> Perhaps above all else, Christianity brought a new conception of humanity to a world saturated with capricious cruelty and the vicarious love of death. . . . What Christianity gave to its converts was nothing less than their humanity.[37]

Today, billions of people in every country on the planet—a network as numerous as the stars in the Abrahamic sky—would declare themselves part of the disciples' legacy and join in their joyful confession that "Jesus is Lord."

THE OLD WAY IS AN EVERYDAY WAY

Because we come to this story through endless layers of history, it's easy to miss how tenuous, how raggedy, how "everyday" it must have been for those living it in real time.

To be sure, Jesus stands alone, and his person is the pivot of history. He was (and is!) Immanuel, God with us, and he has no rival. But consider for a moment how arresting it is that God the Son came as he did—not riding on the clouds of heaven or descending on the temple ablaze with holiness such that everyone would know immediately how exceptional he was. No, he was born in obscurity to a teenage mother and lived for three decades in unrecognizable anonymity.

Though there were of course exceptions, at virtually every turn of his life, Jesus was underestimated. Even after his ministry began, people frequently failed to understand who he was—"though the world was made through him, the world did not recognize him" (John 1:10). During his life, his closest companions consistently struggled to grasp his identity,[38] and even after his resurrection he was mistaken for a gardener (John 20:15), a ghost (Luke 24:37), and a random traveler on the road to Emmaus (Luke 24:13-18). Even when recognized, he consistently embraced an everyday existence like ours, spurning the temptation of celebrity as he directed those who did understand his identity to not disclose who he was (Mark 8:30).

Likewise, though they were used by God in profoundly transformative ways, Jesus' earliest disciples were entirely ordinary kinds of people. They were full of uncertainty and anxiety, marked by fear and failure, and characterized by confusion. Though we mean no irreverence, its simply true that they fumbled their way forward as they followed Jesus in the life of faith.

Seems like we're in good company.

How different, really, was the life of faith in the pages of Acts from what it is today? They too were surrounded by disruption. They were familiar with oppressive systems of exploitation. They too inhabited a compromised religious system. They experienced the full gamut of emotions that also marks our lives—joy and grief, conviction and doubt, connection and isolation. They, like us, were profoundly ordinary and everyday kinds of people, and God used them to change the world.

INTRODUCING THE 4ES

It's this shared everyday reality that makes the lives of Jesus and his first followers such powerful examples for us today. Too often the Western church has embraced a model of faith that relies on religious professionals to provide spiritual "products"—whether an uplifting worship experience or an inspiring sermon—to savvy religious consumers.[39]

In contrast, we believe the new way we need is an old way rooted in the all-play empowerment of everyday people just like we see in the New Testament. When we look more closely at those ancient stories, we see a pattern of reviving mission emerge. It's this pattern we've called the 4*E*s of Reviving Mission—encounter, explore, empower, and establish—that serves as the core paradigm of this book.

Encounter. The reviving mission of Jesus was consistently rooted in *encounter with God*. Whether receiving calling (Luke 3:21-22), reflecting on the Scriptures (Matthew 5:1-7:29), retreating to pray (Mark 1:35), demonstrating the power of God to heal and deliver (Matthew 4:23-25), or consecrating himself through fasting (Luke 4:1-13), Jesus' life was saturated with the wonder that comes from an awareness of God's presence. From beginning to end, the reviving mission of Jesus was sourced in an ongoing encounter with the person of God.

Explore. From that place of encounter, Jesus' regular practice was to *explore what God was doing* wherever he went. He described his own ministry in entirely responsive terms: "The Son can do nothing by himself; he can do only what he sees his Father doing" (John 5:19). In each new community Jesus entered, he looked for people of peace willing to show him hospitality and open their lives to him as hosts for the kingdom of God (Luke 5:27-32). His parabolic teaching was intentionally designed to provoke curiosity and draw those who were hungry out of the crowd (Mark 4:10-25). At every turn, the reviving mission of Jesus was marked by exploring what God was already doing in the people he met and places he inhabited.

Empower. As Jesus recognized the work of God around him, he began to *empower people* by calling them to be with him in discipleship and sent by him in mission. Through invitations like "Come . . . and you will see" (John 1:39), exhortations like "Follow me" (Matthew 4:19), and commands like "Go! I am sending you" (Luke 10:3), Jesus was intentional about calling others to join him and generous in entrusting them with authority as his representatives. Whether through his disciples or transformed individuals like the Samaritan woman (John 4:7-42) and the Gerasene demoniac (Mark 5:19), Jesus' reviving mission was shaped by the ways he empowered everyday people to become ambassadors of the kingdom of God.

Establish. As he empowered others, Jesus was intentional to establish *rhythms of community* that would develop resilience. Whether by cultivating shared habits like prayer (Luke 11:1-4), fasting (Matthew 6:17), and retreat (Mark 6:31), or creating social habitats—distinct groups like the three (Matthew 17:1), the twelve (Mark 3:14), and the seventy-two (Luke 10:1)—Jesus embedded his way in the patterns of everyday life. In so doing, the reviving mission of Jesus grew as he established communal rhythms that would enable ongoing flourishing and fruitfulness.

Though we love the ways the 4Es are rooted deeply in the everyday life of Jesus, what's remarkable is the way they emerge so consistently across the generations of everyday disciples who followed him.

THE 4ES AND JESUS' FIRST DISCIPLES

The sending of the seventy-two in Luke 10 provides a powerful example of the ways this 4*E* framework was transferred to the lives of Jesus' earliest disciples. The story is sourced in *encounter* as Jesus exhorts them to pray and "ask the Lord of the harvest, therefore, to send out workers" (v. 2). As they go, he tells them to *explore* for a house where they would be welcomed (vv. 5-6) and commands them to receive hospitality from these people of peace (vv. 7-8). Further, Jesus *empowers* those he sends with authority (v. 19) and commissions them as ambassadors of the kingdom of God in word, deed, and power (v. 9). Likewise, he uses this opportunity to *establish* rhythms for ministry life as he sends them in partnership ("two by two" in v. 1), in dependence on those to whom they were sent (v. 4), and with a clear emphasis on ministering in households (vv. 4-7). Indeed, it's not a stretch to imagine that these original people of peace in fact became indigenous leaders in a given village—households that became habitats for the kingdom of God.[40]

THE 4ES AND THE EARLY CHURCH

Years later and in an entirely different context, we see this same pattern emerge in the story of Peter and Cornelius in Acts 10. Once again, the story originates in twin *encounters* with God as Cornelius and Peter both receive visions (vv. 3-8 and 9-16). Both respond with *exploration* as Cornelius sends a delegation to look for Peter in Joppa and Peter eagerly travels with that delegation to a new place to look for God at work. Upon his arrival, Peter finds a person of peace (Cornelius) who extends hospitality and whose entire household is primed to receive the good news (vv. 17-29). As Peter is testifying about Jesus, God *empowers* Cornelius and his household with the Holy Spirit and they are baptized in the name of Jesus (vv. 44-48). Throughout the story we see Peter practice some of the same communal rhythms that Jesus had *established* before him—he ministers in community (vv. 23, 45), he practices table fellowship (v. 48), and, as a result, the home of Cornelius the centurion is transformed into an outpost of the kingdom of God.[41]

THE 4ES IN PAUL'S MISSIONARY JOURNEYS

Finally, we see this same pattern repeated in the life of Paul through stories like the one found in Acts 16, where Paul and his companions minister in Philippi. Once again, the origin of the story is *encounter* with God, as Paul receives a vision of a "man of Macedonia" (vv. 6-10). When they arrive in Philippi, Paul and his companions *explore* what God is doing by visiting a place of prayer, where they meet not a Macedonian man but a Turkish woman named Lydia. As a person of peace, Lydia responds to their message and welcomes Paul and his companions into her home (v. 14). In response, they *empower* Lydia by baptizing her (and the whole household where she has influence). Finally, despite the cultural tensions involved in doing so, Paul and his companions stay with Lydia and thereby *establish* a habitat for the gospel in Philippi where believers continued to gather (v. 40).[42]

THE 4ES TODAY

Though these are only a few of the examples we'll examine through the rest of this book, seeing this pattern replicated through the New Testament narrative—especially across different generations of disciples and in contexts as radically distinct as rural Galilee and urban Philippi—grows our conviction that the 4*E*s are a durable model of reviving mission that can serve God's people today.

Though we'll be unpacking these concepts over the coming chapters, here's a simple summary of the 4*E*s that resonates with the scriptural narratives above and outlines a "new but old" way of reviving mission for our day.

Reviving mission is sourced in *encounter* with God's presence and movement around us. Encounter includes traditional spiritual disciplines such as prayer, worship, and Scripture, but it also involves supernatural experiences of calling, healing, and consecration, all of which lead us into deeper wonder and communion with God.

From that foundation of encounter with God, we *explore* what God has done, is doing, and will do in the people and places he's called us to. An essential part of exploring is using curiosity to identify "people of peace" who are receptive to the gospel of the kingdom, relationally connected to a network, and responsive to invitations of obedience.

As we recognize what God is doing in a community, we generously *empower* people. We help them grow their own connection to

God through the Holy Spirit given "without measure," and we serve and send them into his calling on their lives.

Finally, we work alongside those we are empowering to *establish* rhythms of community that grow resilience and support flourishing. Whether habits (everyday practices that embed values) or habitats (the structures and systems that undergird the life of a community), communal rhythms amplify and sustain life over the long haul.

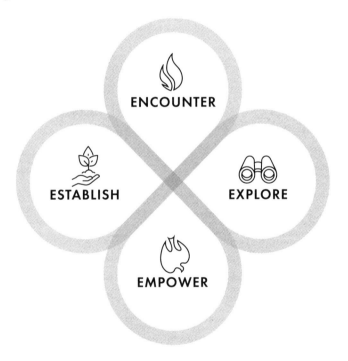

Figure 1.1. The 4*E*s of reviving mission

Over the last decade, God has used the 4*E*s to help hundreds of everyday people awaken to lives of reviving mission and start new faith communities in beautifully distinct contexts around the world. Our conviction is that they are an old way that can be a new way.

Though revivals start with outpourings of God's Spirit, they are sustained when the dynamic movement of God is stewarded through agile, scalable structures—"wineskins" that enable what God is doing to be transferred from one community to the next. Our hope is that now, in light of the new season of revival that we believe is emerging all around us, the 4*E*s might become a "new wineskin" to help steward the everyday movement of God that is being released in our day.

THIS BOOK IS FOR YOU

Regardless of your stage of life, what role you may (or may not) play in a faith community, or where you're at in your spiritual journey, if you want to live a life of holistic faith, this book is for you. If you're wary of expressions of "mission" that feel more like the empire than the kingdom, this book is for you. If you're eager for a simple model of everyday mission to shape the life of your community, this book is for you. If you want to see God's kingdom come in generative ways in your neighborhood or community, this book is definitely for you. And if all you've got is hunger—a longing for God and a desire to be awakened to his everyday movement all around you, this book is most certainly for you, because that's who we are too.

WHO WE ARE

We never set out to be authors. Long before we ever tried to articulate these concepts in chapter outlines or podcast episodes, we were trying to embody these ideas in our lives. As practitioners, we know our first task is not to influence others but to follow Jesus, and it's from that place of imperfect but earnest following that we write.

Together we carry several decades of experience starting new things and leading missional movements. While we got our start in the university world with InterVarsity Christian Fellowship, we've also helped catalyze new work in local church settings and in different countries around the world. Though we've each completed graduate degrees, our heartbeat remains the grassroots work of everyday discipleship. We love empowering people to find their place in God's reviving mission—bearing witness to his goodness in their neighborhoods and families, across workplaces and campus quads.

Though we'll write collectively using "we," "us," and "our" throughout this book, here's some detail on who we are as individuals so you can have a sense of our contexts.

Linson is the associate pastor of METRO Church in Dallas, Texas, where he lives with his wife, Betina, and their two kids, Sophia and JT. He is passionate about serving and reaching the South Asian community in America and around the world. He loves training new leaders, leading teams, and envisioning a new future for the church.

Eric serves as the associate director for planting with InterVarsity/USA and director of groups ministry at his church, One Hope Benson. He loves to help everyday followers of Jesus start new expressions of Jesus' church, especially in overlooked places. He lives in Omaha, Nebraska, with his wife, Stacy, and their three kids, Memo, Elena, and Jonny.

Jon is a vice president for InterVarsity/USA, and he lives in Iowa with his wife, Stephanie, and their two kids, Elijah and Abigail. He is passionate about cultivating missional ecosystems and loves creating the confluence of vision, people, and systems needed to launch and sustain new things.

As missionaries who cut our teeth in the collegiate context, and now as parents of Gen Z children, we feel a sense of urgency to see the church be renewed and a growing sense of hope that God is doing something new in our day. We've tasted of his reviving mission in our own lives and are honored to share some of what we've learned with you.

WHAT'S TO COME

In the next chapter, we'll introduce the second key paradigm of this book—a holistic missiology rooted in the person of God that shapes our postures and our practices. From there we'll work through each *E* over the course of two chapters—encounter (chapters three and four), explore (chapters five and six), empower (chapters seven and eight), and establish (chapters nine and ten). Finally, we'll offer a conclusion and benediction in chapter eleven.

For ease of access, after each couplet of *E* chapters, we'll provide a concise summary and a chart that synthesizes the key concepts we've covered, and we invite you to visit www.revivingmission.org for even more tools and resources.

In the pages that follow, we'll highlight how the 4*E*s are a model for reviving mission that can awaken us to the everyday movement of God. We'll cultivate affection and joy by locating the 4*E*s in the person of God. We'll illustrate how the 4*E*s shape redemptive postures by telling stories of real people living beautiful lives of everyday mission. We'll provide practical tools to help you apply the 4*E*s in your context so you can take your place in the new season God is releasing all around us.

Our hope is that by the end of this book you'll be equipped to recognize the everyday movement of God, inspired by his reviving mission, and moved to deeper worship of the one who is making everything new!

JESUS' HOLISTIC MISSION

AS A TEENAGER, I (Jon) had what you might call a sincere but segmented faith. I had been raised in the church and considered myself a follower of Jesus, but my faith was more of a foundational assumption than a vital experience, more private than public. To be sure, it contributed to my sense of identity and informed my choices, but it was also largely detached from my regular life.

My faith was sequestered to certain times of the week like Sunday morning, reserved for particular places like my church, and limited to specific activities like reading my Bible or praying. My faith wasn't illegitimate; it was just immature and isolated from my everyday experience.

It wasn't until I went to college that this perspective started to shift in a significant way. As I got involved in my campus fellowship, was welcomed into Christian community, and encountered Jesus in the Gospels, I started to awaken to the everyday movement and mission of God all around me. Far more than a personal moral code or a set of private religious practices, faith started to become a life of ongoing friendship with Jesus that mattered as much on Thursday night as it did on Sunday morning.

I still remember gathering in the old chapel in the middle of our campus for "ten o'clock prayer," where our community contended together for the kingdom to come on our campus and interceded for our friends who didn't know Jesus.

Fueled by those prayers, I started to take some first steps of faltering witness in my dorm. I didn't know any better, so I invited everyone I could find to come to a "Bible study" I would be leading on Revelation and Song of Solomon (I wish that were a joke, but it's painfully true). Though I (obviously) had no idea what I was doing, and I'm sure my theology was all wrong, somehow, by the grace of God, dozens of guys from my dorm gathered in the lounge every week to talk about Jesus.

I befriended a guy on my golf team (who would later become my roommate and best man in my wedding). Though he grew up nominally Catholic, he was a deep, curious thinker, and we'd stay up late playing ping-pong and talking about the big questions of life. Though I'm sure it was as much in spite of me as because of me, in the middle of my freshman year, Tim decided to give his life to Jesus, and I got to help baptize him into the family of faith that spring.

Though I had participated in a number of mission trips earlier in my life, for the first time I started to recognize that mission wasn't something unique people in unique places did for God; mission was something God was doing in everyday places through everyday people like me. I began to realize that God was at work reconciling all things and inviting me to join what he was already doing all around me. As I embraced the truth that Jesus' reviving mission is an everyone, everyday reality, it changed my life.

Toward the end of my time on campus, we heard about a growing movement called 24-7 Prayer, and we decided to try to host a twenty-four-hour prayer room on campus for an entire semester.[1] Though I'm still not sure how it happened, the administration miraculously gave us round-the-clock access to a room in the heart of the student union, and our community hosted a relay of night-and-day prayer that lasted from January until May—roughly 2,500 hours of consecutive prayer covered by individuals and small groups from our community. Together we marveled at what God was doing in our midst as dozens of our friends came to faith in Jesus and hundreds were sent as witnesses, whether to their networks of friends or nations around the world.

Awakening to the movement of God in the world around me started to make a difference in me. It energized my relationship with Jesus and transformed my faith. I found myself experiencing a more vibrant spirituality and living in a more ongoing relationship of connection, friendship, and trust. I started to see that spiritual disciplines weren't intended to earn God's love or favor. Rather, those disciplines were to re-center my identity and reconnect me to the source of life. I began to realize that instead of a moral code of dos and don'ts that should be rigidly applied to myself and others, the teachings of Jesus were focused on the internal attitudes and postures of my heart. I started to recognize that if I truly wanted to live a life of integrity, I needed more than mere behavior modification; my heart needed to be formed so that what I did on the outside matched who I was on the inside.

Far from the life of private, segmented faith I had known, awakening to the everyday movement and mission of God infused my whole life. The more I grew in my sense of calling to those around me, the hungrier I became to experience God and embody his way. The more I saw of Jesus, the more I wanted to become like him inside and out.

Though my journey of discipleship is still very much in process, it was during my time in college that I first experienced the transformational power of Jesus' reviving mission, and my life has never been the same.

WE NEED A HOLISTIC WAY FORWARD

Though I didn't realize it at the time, what God initiated during my college experience was an example of the reviving mission of Jesus that sits at the center of this book—a mission that revives both the communities we are sent to and we who are sent.

We are keenly aware of just how broken our world, the church, and our lives are after a season of global crisis that has compounded many of the chronic issues facing our society and the church. Whether in the culture or in our own lives, each of us can recognize the ways our world is desperate for revival.

Unfortunately, too often the church in the West has been far more reactive than redemptive in responding to the disruptions of our day. Instead of contending for renewal, we've allowed ourselves to be co-opted by political agendas. Instead of kingdom mission, we've embraced the colonialism of empire. Instead of a creative reimagination of gospel integrity (which has plenty of room for thoughtful critique), we've settled for a cynical deconstruction of faith. Instead of leadership marked by humble service, we've amplified narcissistic expressions of power that leave a wake of trauma and disillusionment behind them.

Our conviction in writing this book is that the holistic problems we're facing require a holistic solution. We need more than a set of principles that guide our behaviors, more than empty platitudes, and more than quick fixes. We need a fresh, holistic missiology that is sourced in the person of God and that shapes not only our practices but also our postures as sent ones seeking to embody the kingdom in our everyday lives.

We believe the 4*E*s of reviving mission lead us into just this kind of holistic missiology because they resonate with both the ancient way of Jesus and the everyday movement of God emerging all around us.

TOWARD A HOLISTIC MISSIOLOGY

Missiology means "the study of the church's mission,"[2] and in order to understand how the 4*E*s comprise a framework for holistic missiology, we first need to construct something of an etymological bridge through four different languages. So buckle up.

Of course, the linguistic root of *missiology* is *mission*—an English word derived from the Latin *missio*, which means "sending." However, the Bible wasn't written in Latin but mostly in Hebrew and Greek, and it's from those languages that we get the words *shalakh* (Hebrew) and *apostellō* (Greek), each of which are verbs which mean "to send." As you have likely guessed, *apostellō* is also the root for our English word *apostle*, which literally means "sent one." Thus, at the core of a biblical understanding of apostles (or a modern understanding of missionaries) is the concept of sending. Said another way, to live a life of mission is, at a fundamental level, to be sent.

Because mission is all about "sentness," any framework of missiology must speak to our sentness in a dynamic way. David Bosch captures this idea in his book *Transforming Mission* when he says, "The term *mission* presupposes a sender, a person sent by the sender, those to whom one is sent, and an assignment."[3]

As such, the holistic missiology we need must point to who our sending God is, it should reveal how we are called to live as sent people, and it should instruct us in what we are being sent to do.[4] Part of what is so compelling to us about the 4*E*s as a framework for our sentness is the way they speak to these three levels beautifully. Like a master key that unlocks multiple doors, the 4*E*s help us understand who God is as our sender, how we live as sent ones, and what we do as we are sent—a concept we've sought to capture in figure 2.1.

A MODEL OF HOLISTIC MISSIOLOGY

Figure 2.1. The holistic missiology of the 4*E*s

At their core, the 4*E*s help us understand *who God is* as our sender. Far more than a list of steps to accomplish a task or a stale mental paradigm, the 4*E*s are windows into the mystery of God's person. Beholding God in fresh ways is the source of our worship, and each of the 4*E*s reveals the person of God in a way that enables us to experience the reviving mission of Jesus in our own lives.

The 4*E*s also help us understand *how we live* as sent ones. Just as the 4*E*s reveal the mystery of who God is, they also present us with a model for living a lifestyle shaped by kingdom postures that subvert the prevailing culture of our day. Reviving mission in the way of Jesus invites us beyond doing different kinds of things. It invites us to become different kinds of people—people who are marked by integrity and whose lives embody God's redemption.

Finally, the 4*E*s also articulate *what we do* as we are sent into our everyday lives. Just as they reveal the mystery of God and shape a model for how we live, the 4*E*s also articulate a concrete method of reviving mission that helps us practice the everyday movement of God. The 4*E*s are a guide for starting new kingdom communities and living lives of compelling witness wherever he has sent us.

If we are to respond—as individuals and as the people of God—to the profound brokenness of our world and the new season of revival that we see emerging all around us, we need an integrative way forward. We need a fresh articulation of holistic missiology that is rooted in the mystery of who God is as our sender, shapes a model of how we live as sent ones, and informs a method for what we do as we are sent.

As we'll see in the coming chapters, this is precisely what the 4*E*s enable us to do. To help us hold these two frameworks together, at the end of each couplet of chapters, we'll return to a diagram called the reviving mission grid (see figure 2.2) that overlays the 4*E*s of encounter, explore, empower, and establish with the three elements of holistic missiology—who God is, how we live, and what we do.

	WHO GOD IS	HOW WE LIVE	WHAT WE DO
ENCOUNTER God			
EXPLORE what God is doing			
EMPOWER people			
ESTABLISH rhythms of community			

Figure 2.2. Reviving mission grid

LOPSIDED FAITH

Of course, learning to live into a holistic missiology that revives us and the world is a constant challenge, not only for us as authors, but also for us as the collective people of God. If our missiology doesn't hold these three elements together, we will end up with a lopsided faith that compromises our discipleship in a few key ways.

Mystery in isolation: spirituality as abstract experience. Sometimes we overemphasize mystery ("who God is") and fail to embody our spirituality in how we live and what we do. When this happens, we can allow our desire for God to devolve into an insatiable appetite for novel spiritual experiences or the collection of interesting ideas—whether or not they actually translate into our everyday lives. In so doing, we risk valuing information over transformation and the accumulation of experiences over the demonstration of obedience. As a result, we can inadvertently become like the Dead Sea—sterile because it only receives but never releases water.

Model in isolation: formation as self-help spirituality. When we overemphasize model, or how we live, without rooting our formation in who God is and what he calls us to do in the world, we risk allowing our discipleship to Jesus to become just another expression of self-help psychology. In a culture obsessed with health and personal wellness, there is a real temptation to understand Christian spirituality as merely another pathway to personal fulfillment. If we decouple our formation from the person of God and the practices of mission, we can allow obedience to the timeless way of Jesus to be subverted by a gospel of personal wellness that replaces authentic spiritual formation with self-actualization.

Method in isolation: mission as activism. When we allow our method, or what we do, to be decoupled from who God is and how we live, it's easy to settle for a kind of activism that relies on our own strength but is largely devoid of joy, love, and power. No matter how just the cause or how zealous our intent, relying on our own strength as the source of our calling is a sure-fire recipe for personal burnout. Mission understood in this way is like trying to traverse the ocean by the strength of our paddling, rather than hoisting a sail and relying on the power of the wind.

HUNGER FOR HOLISTIC MISSION

Of course, each of these lopsided expressions carries a measure of truth. Holistic mission is certainly about our experience with God, absolutely includes our wellness, and definitely requires our participation. However, the reviving mission of Jesus is so much more than these limited expressions we often settle for in our lives. Any one of these elements—who God is, how we live, or what we do—without the others is like sitting on a stool with two legs or trying to solve a complex mathematical equation using only addition and subtraction.

The lopsided, counterfeit expressions of faith we see within and around us leave us with a weak relationship with God, a fragile sense of self, and a feeble impact in the world. When we fail to allow our awareness of who God is to shape how we live and what we do (and vice versa), we're left with a culture, a church, and a life marked by cynicism instead of wonder, contempt instead of curiosity, narcissism instead of generosity, and fragility instead of resilience.

The needs of the world and the new season God is cultivating require a holistic missiology that incorporates a rich spirituality rooted in the mystery of who God is, a redemptive model of formation that shapes how we live, and a robust method of practice that informs what we do. We believe the 4*Es*—as a holistic framework for our sentness—sit at the nexus of all three of these elements and can help us both awaken to the movement of God and embody the reviving mission of Jesus in our everyday lives.

Though it may be buried below layers of weariness and hidden behind manifold experiences of disappointment, the world's—and our—hunger to experience the holistic, reviving mission of Jesus is real. We yearn for a life of embodied faith that undergirds true flourishing, that energizes true community, and that empowers true impact for the sake of God's mission to reconcile all things. It's as we turn our eyes to Jesus that we find these longings fulfilled, because he is the author and perfecter of just that kind of mission, just that kind of life.

JESUS: HOLISTIC MISSION EMBODIED

We are compelled by the ways the 4Es are rooted in the person and life of Jesus. More than being merely our savior, Jesus is our example for how to live a life of holistic, reviving mission. He is the one who shows us how our sentness can shape our understanding of who God is, how we live, and what we do in integrated ways. Whenever we get out of balance and start to live a lopsided faith, it is returning to the life of Jesus that helps us reorient our lives, and it's in his person that we see this model of holistic mission fully embodied.

Who God is: "I am the one who was sent." One of the most striking themes of the Gospels is the way Jesus refers to himself and to God, because it gives us a window into how Jesus allowed his sentness to shape his spirituality—his experience of who God is.

Jesus uses a variety of self-descriptions throughout the Gospel of John—beautiful metaphors such as the "good shepherd" (John 10), the "true vine" (John 15), and "the bread of life" (John 6). However, one of the most common ways Jesus describes himself in this Gospel is as "a sent one" and he consistently calls God "the one who sent me." Indeed, more than forty times in twenty-one chapters Jesus uses some combination of these phrases to describe either his identity or that of his Father.

Though these are only a few of the references, consider for a moment the ways these passages help us see just how central Jesus' sense of mission was to his understanding of who God is.

"My food," said Jesus, "is to do the will of him who sent me and to finish his work." (John 4:34)

And the Father who sent me has himself testified concerning me. You have never heard his voice nor seen his form, nor does his word dwell in you, for you do not believe the one he sent. (John 5:37-38)

Jesus answered, "The work of God is this: to believe in the one he has sent." (John 6:29)

Then Jesus cried out, "Whoever believes in me does not believe in me only, but in the one who sent me. The one who looks at me is seeing the one who sent me." (John 12:44-45)

Now this is eternal life: that they know you, the only true God, and Jesus Christ, whom you have sent. (John 17:3)

Far from being something auxiliary or extra, Jesus located his sentness at the very core of who he was—"I am the sent one"—and who he understood God to be—"the one who sent me." As such, Jesus' sentness shaped not only his assignment but his spirituality, not just his calling but his identity. Mission wasn't just something Jesus did; it was who he was and who he understood God to be. Jesus' sentness was essential to his spirituality, and his understanding of God as "the Father who sent me" shaped the whole of his life.

This same thing is true for us. We too are sent by the triune God—Father, Son, and Holy Spirit—with more than a missional calling; we too have a missional identity. Just like Jesus, our sentness must shape our spirituality, and our understanding of who God is must overflow into how we live and what we do.

How we live: Jesus knew. One of the final accounts of Jesus' earthly life, when he washed his disciples' feet in John 13, gives us a powerful window into the ways Jesus allowed his sentness to shape how he lived.

The passage highlights the ways that Jesus' posture of servanthood was rooted in what he knew to be true. John 13:3 makes it clear that Jesus not only knew his own authority ("the Father had put all things under his power") but he also was keenly aware of his sentness ("he had come from God and was returning to God").

However, Jesus didn't allow this knowledge of his sentness to be sequestered as an abstract theological construct. No, he lived his truths. Jesus allowed the fullness of these mysteries—the things he knew about God and himself—to be translated into how he lived. As he disrobed, wrapped himself in a towel, held the basin, and washed the grit and grime off his disciples' feet, his life became an embodied parable of his sentness that revealed the fullness of his love for them and the world he would soon send them to serve.

Though the disciples were profoundly confused by what he was doing, Jesus was clear that this embodied demonstration of how he lived was in fact an invitation for how *they* were to live.

> I have set you an example that you also should do as I have done to you. Very truly I tell you, slaves are not greater than their master, nor are messengers greater than the one who sent them. If you know these things, you are blessed if you do them. (John 13:15-17 NRSVUE)

This same invitation stands for us. Just as Jesus allowed what he knew to shape how he lived, we, too, are invited to live our truths. We are to follow Jesus' example and allow our sentness to be translated into lives of embodied integrity.

***What we do: authority and* exousia.** In similar fashion, Jesus' sentness also shaped what he did. As we'll discuss later, at the very heart of Jesus' ministry was the empowerment of the Holy Spirit. Just as the Father sent the Spirit upon Jesus at his baptism, so the Spirit sent Jesus into his ministry (Luke 3:22 and 4:14). Indeed, the whole of Jesus' ministry—what he did—was shaped by the power of the missionary (i.e., sent and sending) Holy Spirit within him.

Closely related to Jesus' power (which in Greek is the word *dynamis*, from which we derive the English word "dynamite") is the idea of Jesus' authority. We see the extraordinary nature of Jesus' authority in passages such as Mark 1:22, which says, "The people were amazed at his teaching, because he taught them as one who had authority, not as the teachers of the law." The Greek word for "authority" here is *exousia*, which is a combination of the prefix *ex-*, which means "out of," and *ousia*, which means "essence or true being." As such, the word translated here as "authority" can rightly be understood as meaning something like "out of one's true being."

Jesus' ministry—what he did—was so amazing because it was marked by a kind of authority sourced not *externally* (like the teachers of the law), but *internally*, from the presence of the sent and sending Spirit within him. Jesus' mission emerged "out of his true being"—the power to do what he did was sourced in his sentness. It was as he allowed the Holy Spirit in him to flow through him that he ministered in authority.

Just as what Jesus did was rooted in his sentness, so too is this true for us as his people. Ultimately, any authority we have is strictly derivative. It's only when we align our lives with Jesus' life and allow the sent and sending Holy Spirit *in* us to move *through* us that we can truly walk in the authority Jesus promised us to do the things he did.

We love the ways Jesus embodied a holistic missiology and allowed his understanding of who God was, how he lived, and what he did to be fundamentally shaped by his sentness—Jesus didn't just *have* a mission, he *was* mission—his sentness saturated every part of his existence.

We are compelled by the ways this kind of holistic missiology might transform our lives, our culture, and our communities. How much more vibrant might our spirituality be if we embraced the sentness of Jesus and allowed our understanding of who God is to awaken us to his everyday movement all around us?

How might our culture shift if we, the body of Christ, were known not as people of judgmental hypocrisy—whose lives do not match their words—but rather as people of holistic integrity—trusted because the way we live embodies the truth of what we believe?

How might our communities change if we walked in the authority of Jesus—empowered to do what he did through surrendering to the missionary Spirit within us?

In the midst of this new season emerging all around us, we believe God is calling his people to embrace the kind of holistic mission we see in Jesus himself. He is the original sent one, and it is only his reviving mission that can renew our hearts and transform our world.

REVIVING MISSION IN EVERYDAY LIFE —NAOMI'S STORY

As we close this chapter, we'd like to share a story about a young woman named Naomi, who is a powerful example of how Jesus' holistic, everyday mission can revive both individuals and entire communities.

Naomi grew up in a family of faith, and her parents were constantly bringing her along to church—she jokes that she was "there every day!" However, as she prepared to graduate from high school, she found herself feeling increasing pressure to keep up appearances and maintain her reputation. Slowly, she slid into a season of compromise where her actions did not match her words and she found her once-vibrant faith eroding and becoming lopsided.

After high school she attended a local community college where she was invited to a campus faith community. There, she experienced a revitalization of her relationship with God that immediately led her into expressions of holistic mission where she allowed her sentness to shape her understanding of who God was, how she lived, and what she did. She would later testify, "My self-centered relationship with God became so much bigger than me." She began to pray for her classmates and lead a Bible study of her own particularly geared for other Black students on campus, even in the midst of Covid-19 lockdowns.

Though she had planned to transfer to a university in Florida, God had other ideas, and she sensed him calling her to enroll in a small private school in her hometown that was known to be resistant to faith communities. Despite that resistance, during her first year on this new campus she started another faith community for Black students. Through her efforts and the blessing of God, the community eventually grew to involve more than twenty people, and Naomi had the privilege of leading one of her friends to faith in Jesus.

Though the Lord had already been using her in powerful ways, he had much more planned for Naomi during her final semester on campus in the spring of 2023. In reflecting on the story, she remembers God calling her to "reach further" by trying to start yet another faith community on campus—this one a Bible study that would bring students of different ethnicities together.

After a month of trying to launch the new community, Naomi was in a rough spot—she was overwhelmed by the demands of her final semester and depressed by what seemed like minimal spiritual momentum in her own life and the lives of those around her. However, in contrast to her season of compromise in high school, Naomi decided to contend for breakthrough. She avoided the temptation to hide what was happening in her life and devoted herself to seeking God holistically with honesty, transparency, and a sincere faith.

After a particularly meaningful time of prayer, she sensed God extending her an invitation to "fast and pray." Rather than responding to this word in an individual way, she felt compelled to rally her community to join her in seven days of communal fasting and prayer for revival on campus. Remarkably, in the timing of God, that season of fasting started just three days after the culmination of the outpouring at Asbury that we wrote about in the preface!

Though we're sure only Jesus knows the full story, what God did through Naomi's obedience was nothing short of remarkable.

Over the course of the week of fasting, student leaders from multiple ministries joined together in fervent worship and intercession for their campus. Each night more and more students joined in. What had started as a small community of roughly a dozen students began to swell, and the small chapel where they were meeting became a place of corporate encounter not unlike Hughes Auditorium at Asbury.

In the midst of this experience, Naomi sensed another invitation from God to be baptized as an embodied symbol of the new life God had given her. But once again this wasn't just an invitation for her; it became an invitation for her community.

After seven days of corporate fasting, worship, and prayer, God broke through. Not only was Naomi baptized in the middle of campus while surrounded by more than two hundred people, but she was also joined spontaneously by twenty other students who decided to give their lives to Jesus and join her in the waters of baptism, right there on the campus quad!

In reflecting on the experience, one of Naomi's mentors, Tyler, had this to say: "After baptisms, we worshiped like never before with only three songs—this wasn't a 'production of hype'—just worship to Jesus. Then other students, a high schooler, and some community members shared testimonies for more than three hours of God's work in their lives!"

The week after the baptisms, the spiritual atmosphere of the campus had shifted. A new generation of leaders had been raised up to continue ministering on campus. The same administration that had previously been resistant to faith communities gave approval to a student to pass out Bibles in the university commons. Students in every building on campus could be found with Bibles open, sharing testimonies, and laying hands on one another in prayer!

Jesus' reviving mission changed Naomi's life and the life of her community, and we love the ways her story is a powerful example of both the 4*E*s and holistic mission at work.

Throughout her time in college, Naomi made encounter with God a priority through fasting, worship, and prayer. She was constantly exploring what he was doing wherever he sent her, starting new faith communities even when it didn't fit into her plans. In response to God's invitation, she rallied her community and empowered others to experience God for themselves by helping them connect to the Holy Spirit. Together they established rhythms of community—habits and habitats—that God used to bring renewal to an entire campus!

What's more, we can also see the ways her engagement with those 4*E*s formed her in a life of holistic mission rooted in her sentness. Her awareness of who God is expanded as she responded to his calling on her life. How she lived changed as she contended for breakthrough instead of sliding into compromise. What she did carried the authority of integrity as Jesus used her obedience to catalyze a movement of fasting, prayer, and witness that transformed the life of her community and the spiritual climate of her university!

As this new season continues to emerge in our midst, we believe there are more stories like Naomi's waiting to be lived (and told) around the world. What is God stirring in you that might also be an invitation for your community? Where are you being awakened to his everyday movement? How might God want to move through you to express his reviving mission where he has sent you?

4Es — **ENCOUNTER** — EXPLORE — EMPOWER — ESTABLISH

ENCOUNTER

God Is Here

IT WAS THE END OF THE FALL SEMESTER. It felt like everyone had disappeared from campus except the depressed engineering students. Many of us were cramming for our final exams in the dungeons of the library. I (Linson) decided I could not retain any more information and started walking back to my dorm.

As I walked across the campus alone, I contemplated the past semester. It was a rare crisp, cold evening in Austin, Texas. I could see my breath appear and disappear in the quiet darkness of the campus.

Much like the fleeting puffs of breath, my semester felt like it had started and vanished in a moment. But there were some lingering moments of regret, shame, loneliness, and cynicism as I considered my time.

Despite growing up as a Christian, a few riveting philosophy classes had led me to start wrestling with the idea of becoming an atheist. What I learned in those classes unexpectedly disrupted my entire framework of faith, and though I wasn't yet convinced, I slowly began laying down the underpinnings of a very different kind of worldview.

As I turned down the last corner toward my dorm, a deep sense of isolation filled me. I was far from family, friends, and God. I knew these thoughts of loneliness shouldn't surprise me, but they settled on me in a fresh way, like the dark of night all around me. I felt deeply alone.

I entered my dorm room and lay down on my lumpy bed, looking for excuses not to study. I was surprised when Bible stories from my childhood began to fill my head: Joseph alone in Egypt, Daniel alone in the lions' den, Jesus alone at Gethsemane, Paul and Silas alone in prison.

As I considered these stories, I realized I hadn't actually read my Bible since arriving on campus, primarily because of the cynicism growing in my heart toward religion and religious people. But at that moment, something compelled me to read it.

I can't explain why or how it happened. I got up, went over to my desk, and searched for my Bible. There it was, under a pile of junk, paperwork, and fast food receipts. It had been there for so long the leather cover had bonded itself to my desk. I pulled on it. Hard.

When my parents had moved me into my dorm, they had given me this Bible as a graduation gift. It was beautiful. My name was engraved on the front. My dad had gone through each book and highlighted his favorite verses. I could still hear his confident, strong voice in my head. "Son, if you get lost or feel defeated, just open this Bible and read something I highlighted."

I wiped away the dust and opened it for the first time. Perhaps it was a prayer, or a thought, or just a fleeting wish, but I whispered, "God, I have no idea if you are real anymore, but if you are, here's your chance. I need help."

I started flipping through the pages of that Bible. My eyes raced to the highlighted Scriptures, desperate for a sign from God. I found many of the highlighted verses to be interesting, but they weren't what I needed. I kept going from page to page, then book to book. As I came to the end of the Bible, I saw I had reached

Revelation. At this point my hope was waning that God was going to speak to me. Perhaps this was all just a waste of time to avoid studying?

Then my eyes came across a highlighted passage that stopped me in my tracks. It was Revelation 3:15-16: "You are neither cold nor hot. I wish you were either one or the other! So, because you are lukewarm—neither hot nor cold—I am about to spit you out of my mouth."

I stared at those verses. Though I was reading the Bible, it felt like it was reading me.

I felt a warm sensation come across my body and my eyes filled with tears. I realized how lukewarm I had become. I felt the isolation, shame, and cynicism I carried every day creeping back in. Memories crashed together in my mind and heart, and I heard myself say, "I'm so sorry, Jesus." Reality hit me hard.

Like a flood, I felt Jesus' presence fill my empty dorm room. I wept. It was as if Jesus was standing in my room and embracing me. I couldn't believe how real it all felt. It felt so surprising, but at the same time so intentional, that it was almost like Jesus had been patiently planning this moment all my life.

It filled me with wonder that Jesus was here with me. Jesus found me in a city away from home. Jesus filled my lonely dorm room. Jesus freed me from being trapped by sin, isolation, and cynicism.

That encounter with Jesus changed my life.

WONDER THAT COMES FROM ENCOUNTERING GOD

This is a book about the reviving mission of Jesus—a fresh articulation of mission that helps us awaken to the everyday movement of God all around us. It is a call to take our place in his mission to revive a profoundly broken world. However, before we can talk about revival "out there," we need to talk about revival "in here," and revival always starts in a place of encounter with God—much like the one I had in my dorm room.

The trick is that it's easy for us to get lulled into believing God is far away, unconcerned, or too busy. But God is here, right now. With you and me.

Even while you read this book.

Before we move on, take a moment to be still and open yourself to an encounter with God. Take a couple of slow, deep breaths. Tell him you want to experience his presence. Invite him to renew your wonder.

• • •

Just as was true in my story, unless we're intentional about seeking God and receiving the wonder that comes from encounter, our hearts tend toward cynicism. Particularly after the disruption of the last few years, cynicism is rampant.

Research has shown that cynicism breeds negativity and pessimism. It drains energy from joyful activities, undermines our connections with others, and breeds distrust of people and systems.[1] Cynicism strangles our souls. We see it all around us—in our schools, in our workplaces, in our politics, in our families, and in our churches. If we're honest, we also see it in ourselves.

So, what do we do?

Dacher Keltner, author and UC Berkeley professor, believes there is hope for our societal cynicism if we can experience wonder. He states, "Being in a context of awe leads to a 'small self.' We can quiet that nagging voice of the interfering neurotic simply by locating ourselves in contexts of more awe."[2]

Isn't it fascinating when science confirms what the Scriptures have always suggested—the antidote to cynicism is experiencing awe and being in spaces that cultivate wonder.[3]

As Christians, we know having an encounter with God is the best way to reintroduce ourselves to the "small self." As we magnify

God, we give him a larger space in our lives. As we direct our gaze toward him, we begin to see ourselves and our situations in their appropriate place, and we experience the wonder that can soften our cynical hearts.

Mike Cosper, director of the podcast *The Rise and Fall of Mars Hill*, calls us to recapture our wonder despite the overwhelming cynicism we might feel about American Christianity. Cosper suggests we can cultivate a posture of expectancy through paying attention to the enchanted world around us and recognizing that our daily lives are laced with potential to encounter God.[4]

For many of us that posture feels new. Do you have that kind of expectancy in your daily, ordinary life? Could you possibly encounter God as you converse with a coworker, make your daily commute to work, study for a final exam, or clean up your child's room (again)? Is the world truly "enchanted" with the presence of God? We believe that it is, and that recognizing it can rescue us from our cynical isolation.

As we turn our attention toward God and consider the works of his hands (Psalm 8:3), we begin to feel the transforming power of his presence. As we reorient our lives toward expectancy, our wonder grows and the seed of cynicism dies. We're set free from the influences of an increasingly pessimistic and melancholy society. As we encounter God and experience wonder, he begins to renew our own hearts and we taste the revival we testify about.

THE PRESENCE OF GOD

The "presence of God" is a well-worn phrase. We hear it in sermons and see it in books, but what does it actually mean to encounter the presence of God?

The Scriptures are full of descriptions of the presence of God inhabiting creation. The prophets declare:

> It is he who sits above the circle of the earth,
> > and its inhabitants are like grasshoppers;
> who stretches out the heavens like a curtain,
> > and spreads them like a tent to dwell in. (Isaiah 40:22 ESV)

The psalmist adds:

> Where can I go from your Spirit?
> > Where can I flee from your presence?
> If I go up to the heavens, you are there;
> > if I make my bed in the depths, you are there.
> If I rise on the wings of the dawn,
> > if I settle on the far side of the sea,
> even there your hand will guide me,
> > your right hand will hold me fast. (Psalm 139:7-10)

Though we know that God is always present, these Scriptures also suggest that his presence is boundless and too great for us to comprehend. This is a theological concept called transcendence, which means that God, while entirely present, is also beyond our experience or perception.[5] Though he made everything, he is far above all that he has created.

Yet simultaneously, God chooses to be connected, concerned, and close to what he has created. He reveals himself to us. He comes near. Scripture repeatedly reminds us of his nearness: "The Lord is near to all those who call on him" (Psalm 145:18 ESV); "The Lord is near to the brokenhearted" (Psalm 34:18 ESV); "He is . . . not far from each one of us" (Acts 17:27 ESV); "Draw near to God, and he will draw near to you" (James 4:8 ESV). Despite his surpassing greatness, God's very nature is to be close to us. More than we desire to be with him, God desires to be with us in every moment of our lives. This is a theological truth that we know as his immanence.[6] As hard as it is to imagine, God is close to you and me, even at this very moment.

However, there are also moments in Scripture where God's presence seems intensified and manifest in a unique way. Since we know that God's presence with us is constant, what actually changes in these moments is our awareness, as we are suddenly awakened to his nearness and hereness. In these moments—just like the moment I (Linson) had in my dorm room—we are sensitive to the presence of God and we feel humility, wonder, and closeness. We experience God's manifest, right-there-with-us presence that fills us with an impulse to respond to him in obedience.

We see these kinds of experiences throughout the scriptural narrative, from Abraham hearing from God to leave his people and country (Genesis 12) to Moses at the burning bush (Exodus 3) to Joshua meeting the commander of the Lord's armies (Joshua 5) to Elijah hearing the whisper of God (1 Kings 19) to the angel Gabriel visiting Mary (Luke 1) to the disciples witnessing Jesus' transfiguration (Mark 9) to Paul's encounter with Jesus on the road to Damascus (Acts 9).

It is incredible to see the nature of God shining through each of these encounters. God comes near to humanity, literally face-to-face with us: men and women, Jews and Gentiles, the powerful and the marginalized, young and old. We see the undeniable truth that God is willing to meet with anyone, in any place, at any time. He loves us and is ready for an encounter with us!

But, while we can never lose the reality of God's presence, we can lose our awareness of his nearness. Therefore, we should deeply desire to encounter him as often as we can, to be awakened by him, to be close to him, and to be sent by his words. Sometimes it's simply recognizing and articulating our longing for God that can help us awaken to his presence. Do not be afraid, cynical, or distant, because with the groaning of even one unintelligible prayer, the triune God can awaken you and me to the powerful and surprising reality of his movement.

From dorm rooms in Austin, Texas, to ancient Near East deserts in the Old Testament, to an upper room in Jerusalem, to urban city centers, to rural counties all across the nation and the globe, God is with us and wants to speak to us. Would you consider longing for this kind of encounter so you can experience the reviving mission of Jesus?

WE ARE GOING TO ANOTHER REVIVAL MEETING?

Growing up, I (Linson) did not like the word *revival*. I guess you could say I was skeptical about revivals. I felt like most of the youth groups in my city (including my own) were filled with "youth camp junkies." We would go to these camps and gain a spiritual high and then come back totally unchanged. We talked about this incredible experience, but nothing seemed different about us or our friends.

I remember during one of these camps, a student went down to the altar and seemed to have some kind of spiritual experience. But later than night, while we were all back in the cabins, he bragged about how far he had gotten with some of the girls attending camp. It felt sleazy and incongruent with what had transpired earlier that evening at the altar. It seemed like he was jumping from experience to experience—trying to make his buzz last.

My cynicism would have grown except I did notice that some other folks at the camp matured over time into strong believers. Some started to become leaders. Others had a winsome way of bringing their friends closer to God. I had to admit, they were actually very different. They seemed like they were revived. Their encounters produced not just experience but obedience. But why? What was I missing?

GOD IS THE PRIMARY FOCUS OF ENCOUNTER

Simon Sinek, author and speaker, has a popular TED talk and book titled *Start with Why*. His signature premise is that "why" matters more than "what" or "how."[7] Essentially, Sinek explains, good organizations cannot focus merely on what they are making or selling, or even how efficiently or perfectly they make it, but they must know why they make it. For Sinek, "why" is primary before anything else.

We agree—we must know why we long to have an encounter with God. Is it because we want something supernatural to happen to us? Or because we want to experience something therapeutic? Or because we do not want to be left out of what others are experiencing?

Most of these desires are not bad, but they do run the risk of centering ourselves and not God. Often we make ourselves the center of experiences. But the results or outcomes of that type of arrangement are minimal and short-lived. Who is truly at the center of our spiritual experiences? Are we seeking God or are we centering ourselves?

We believe we must take Sinek's argument down one more layer from "what," "how," and "why" to "who." "Who" matters infinitely more than we think. Yes, having a spiritual experience is good, but the main focus—the main "why," the main "who"—must be God himself. We have all read about churches and nonprofits that have a meaningful "why"—a strong vision and mission—but too often, many of these same churches and organizations collapse because they were all about their senior pastor or leader. They were building on the wrong "who."

We believe this is the main difference between those who collect spiritual experiences but remain unchanged and those who truly have an encounter with God and then live differently. The latter have made God the center by seeking him first. Our spirituality and motivation for mission are based not simply on an experience; they are based in the person of God. We know that God's nature is to meet with us, but do we truly desire to meet with him? Or do we just want another spiritual high?

It may feel strange at first, but shifting our attention to God is transformative. In conversation and prayer with students and young adults from my church, I (Linson) have witnessed anxiety released and cynicism subverted when they recognize that the spotlight of life and mission is on God and not on them. The realization that they were not the main character of life gave them permission to surrender before God. By surrendering to God, they made him their primary "who"—he was magnified to his rightful place in their lives. He gave them the desire to trust and obey. They were free to respond to his initiative.

Mark Sayers, author and pastor, helps us here when he states, "There is a deep sense that millions have fallen into the contemporary pattern of life, one of continual consumption, ever-present anxiety, and self-focus—an unsustainable pattern. Many are realizing that what they long for can only be satisfied by the eternal God."[8] It is true; only God can satisfy us. We can break free from this consumeristic, anxious, damaging pattern only if we take the focus off ourselves and seek after God. As we seek him (and not just our experiences), our anxieties lower, our cynicism dissipates, our awe increases, and our calling toward mission grows. These are the signs of a true encounter with God.

In an age when social media asks us to take center stage, make a scene, draw comments and likes, and become a carefully curated version of ourselves, it's a breath of fresh air to know that all of that is unnecessary. We are supporting characters in this story of life. In truth, we are more like anonymous extras on set. God is the star. God receives all our focus. We must embrace the truth that all transformational encounters are about God, not us. In this place of true encounter, we are revived in our sense of mission and calling and empowered to join Jesus' reviving mission.

THE PRESENCE OF GOD AT PENTECOST

As we mentioned earlier, we named this book *Reviving Mission* because we believe that the mission of Jesus revives not only the places we are sent to, but us as sent ones. We cannot give something we haven't received, and we hope you are finding your hunger to seek God's revival in your own life stoked.

But encountering God's presence doesn't merely revive us. Rather, God's presence also empowers us to become carriers of God's reviving presence wherever we go—something that became possible when God moved even closer to his people at Pentecost in Acts 2.

When the Holy Spirit came upon the believers gathered in the upper room, the creative Spirit that hovered over the waters of chaos at creation took up residence in a community. The Advocate, the Counselor, the Spirit of Truth, and the Gift promised by Jesus and his Father moved into their very lives. What's more, through Jesus, we too can become temples for the Holy Spirit such that God's presence inhabits our lives and we can live in permanent encounter with him.

We love the way that Michael Heiser, Old Testament scholar and author, captures the implications of this moment: "Believe it or not, you are sacred space ... the place where God now tabernacles—we are the temple of God, both individually and corporately."[9] Though it may be strange to think about our lives as "sacred space," it also matches the logical progression of the scriptural narrative. From beginning to end, God has been drawing near to his people so that he might dwell with (and in) them. God literally resides in us—our lives are a place of ongoing encounter with the triune God. Incredible!

Why is this encounter so important?

It's striking to reflect on how Jesus spoke to his disciples before his ascension when he told them, "Do not leave Jerusalem, but wait for the gift my Father promised" (Acts 1:4).

Think about all the disciples had in that moment. They had followed Jesus for three years, listening to every sermon and witnessing countless miracles. They had experienced his forgiveness for their failures and the transformation of their community. They had been trained by him to teach and heal and deliver. And they had witnessed his resurrection (they were literally talking with the resurrected Jesus in that moment!).

What else could they possibly need? Surely that was enough to compel them into mission, right? Not according to Jesus. He makes it clear they are not to "go." In fact, he gives them two commands in this passage, both of which are the opposite of "go": "Do not leave" and "wait."

Why wouldn't Jesus want the disciples to go and testify about him as quickly as possible? Because at Pentecost, when the Holy Spirit comes on their community, God births the church—this encounter is the bedrock of their sentness. At Pentecost the Holy Spirit not only encounters the disciples; the Holy Spirit inhabits the disciples, and that releases an incredible impulse to go into all the world. Just as we see throughout the rest of the scriptural narrative, this encounter with the presence of God creates wonder and a willingness to trust and obey God more deeply. Despite great persecution and obstacles, the disciples move from that place of encounter with God into embodied action as carriers of the reviving Spirit of God.

When we think about reviving mission, it's easy to fall into the same trap of assuming we are the "main characters" of mission. It's easy to think mission is mainly about our action, our obedience, our zeal. It's easy to believe that God is somehow waiting on us or that mission is something we do for God.

However, the good news of a reviving mission rooted in encounter is that mission isn't about us; it's about God. Mission isn't something we do for God; it's something God is doing through us, and that distinction makes all the difference. Unless it's rooted in an encounter with the person and movement of God—indeed, unless we make our lives a dwelling place for God—mission quickly devolves into an exercise in our own effort.

But when we recognize that God is the main character of mission—when we root not just our encounter but our calling in the right "who"—everything changes. God is the one who leads mission. All we have to do is hoist our sail and follow his lead.

SEEKING TO ENCOUNTER GOD TODAY

If God is always near to us and longs to encounter us and inhabit our lives so we can become carriers of his presence and partners in his mission, how should we respond? Whether we're seeking our own revival or the revival of our communities, Scripture reminds us we must seek after God.

The Old Testament underscores our role as seekers. The author of Deuteronomy states, "You will seek the LORD your God and you will find him, if you search after him with all your heart and with all your soul" (Deuteronomy 4:29 ESV). David embodies this posture when he states in the Psalms,

> O God, you are my God; earnestly I seek you;
> > my soul thirsts for you;
> my flesh faints for you,
> > as in a dry and weary land where there is no water.
> > > (Psalm 63:1 ESV)

King Solomon, Isaiah, and Jeremiah also call the people of God to seek after him diligently (Proverbs 8:17; Isaiah 55:6; Jeremiah 29:13). Throughout the Old Testament we see a pattern of God inviting his people to yearn and seek after his presence in their lives.

Jesus picks up this same theme in his Sermon on the Mount, where he says, "But seek first the kingdom of God and his righteousness. . . . Ask, and it will be given to you; seek, and you will find; knock, and it will be opened to you. For everyone who asks receives, and the one who seeks finds, and to the one who knocks it will be opened" (Matthew 6:33; 7:7-8 ESV). Clearly Jesus knew that the secret to knowing the Father was to seek out his presence in our daily lives. The question becomes, will we seek God with this type of importance and urgency?

We seek God because we know he can be found. Though God is not hidden, often his movement is subtle, and the static of cynicism makes it hard to detect his presence. But he is making himself available to us if we will turn our hearts toward him and resist the distractions around us. Though seeking God will require offering our time, attention, and energy, finding God in the place of encounter and carrying his reviving presence everywhere we go makes it all worth it.

Here are three particular ways we can seek God so we can be awakened to his everyday movement in us and join in his reviving mission around us.

SEEK GOD THROUGH ATTENTION

Dallas Willard, theologian and philosopher, says, "The first act of love is the giving of attention."[10] We believe this is a critical starting point for encounter, and in fact, offering God our focused attention is a type of praying, even before we speak a single word to God.

Set aside some time to reflect in silence, as silence often helps cultivate attentiveness. If this is new to you, start with five minutes and increase it over time. Put away your devices and other distractions. Don't worry about making everything perfect. Our minds will drift. Our affections will be allured by many things. Our imaginations will roam without our permission. We must accept that this is just the way it is and we're learning as we go. Be patient and bring yourself back to quiet attention.

I (Linson) have found that walking outdoors or sitting at a local park helps me cultivate my attentiveness. As I reflect on God's work in creation, in people, in communities, and in systems, I begin to understand the psalmist's declaration in Psalm 104 that every part of creation declares the greatness and faithfulness of God. I experience the nearness of his presence as I see his fingerprint on all things.

Sometimes I'll also use a practice called lectio divina, which is prayerfully reading the Scriptures as you pay attention to the voice of the Spirit.[11] I have spent several days, even weeks, on one chapter in the Bible—reading, rereading, praying, listening, and memorizing the verses of Scripture as his presence washed over me. It can feel dry at first, but over time I have found my imagination illuminated, my heart melted, and my spiritual being quickened in surprising ways. Soaking in Scripture helps me be attentive to the presence of God with and around me.

Spending time in silence, walking outdoors or sitting at a park, or practicing the spiritual discipline of lectio divina are all starting points for an active, ongoing life of encounter with God. However, we are all wired differently, so I encourage you to try various spiritual disciplines and activities—God may surprise you as he awakens you to his movement all around you.

Jon Tyson, pastor of Church of the City in New York, has said that "God comes where he is wanted. Hunger is the key."[12] In a culture swimming in distraction, perhaps it is our willingness to silence all other voices and give our attention to God that is the best indicator of our hunger for him.

SEEK GOD THROUGH CONSECRATION

Consecration helps us recognize that we are set apart, different, and made holy by God. Consecration is when we set aside extended time to fast, pray, or abstain from activities that might distract us or deter our desire for God's presence in our lives.

We realize that fasting is no easy task, especially when it is connected to spiritual breakthrough. It is uncanny how often people offer me doughnuts when I (Linson) am in a season of fasting! But fasting reminds me that I must consciously resist that urge and place my hope and trust in God as my source of true well-being. I have friends who have made the decision to stop drinking alcohol or stop eating meat or sweets for extended periods of time until they encountered a breakthrough in the presence of God.

Though fasting is about abstention from physical things, Dallas Willard reminds us of the spiritual provision released during fasting when he states, "Fasting is done that we may consciously experience the direct sustenance of God to our body and our whole person."[13] Willard knows that the presence of God sustains us far more powerfully than food and drink ever could if we are willing to step into consecration.

We need to remember that God told Joshua and the people of Israel, "Consecrate yourselves, for tomorrow the Lord will do amazing things among you" (Joshua 3:5). The next day they trusted and obeyed God as they crossed through the Jordan on dry ground—even during its flood stage—and entered the Promised Land. What kind of breakthrough might await you and your community on the other side of consecration?

SEEK GOD THROUGH CONTENDING PRAYER

We realize that the intensity of contending prayer is not for everyone, and we understand that we all have different church traditions and backgrounds. But as a Pentecostal, South Asian American, I (Linson) would be remiss if I did not mention this spiritual practice. It is a key part of how my community encounters the presence of God, both individually and communally.

This type of prayer posture might feel new or not what you want to do right away, and that's okay. But let me explain how this discipline has been critical to my personal moments of encounter with God.

What is contending prayer? It is a posture in prayer that feels markedly different from a typical prayer time with God. Most of us may be more familiar with contemplative prayer, breath prayer, liturgical prayer, and so forth, which are all incredibly valuable. But there are times in life that the intensity, focus, duration, and commitment to prayer is much higher and more intense. Some would say this kind of prayer moves from seeking to knocking.

For example, my church will engage in twenty-one days of fasting and prayer for our church every January. We spend time in focused intercession. We lean into the authority given to us by Christ through the finished work of the cross and stand firm despite any kind of spiritual disruption or warfare. We pray until we are changed or the situation around us has changed. This posture of prayer leads our community into humility, dependency, and fervency.

British evangelist and Harvard lecturer Rodney "Gypsy" Smith describes this kind of prayer by stating, "Go home, lock yourself in your room. Kneel down in the middle of the floor, and with a piece of chalk, draw a circle around yourself. There, on your knees, pray fervently and brokenly that God would start a revival within that chalk circle."[14] Furthermore, James the brother of Jesus states that the fervent, passionate prayers of righteous people accomplish much (James 5:16). Something happens—something is accomplished—when we move into this posture of prayer. This posture of contending keeps pressing forward, not giving up, seeking passionately, until there is a breakthrough—an encounter with God.

Will you consider taking a step toward an encounter with God? Will you offer your attention by making space in your life for silent reflection? Like Naomi in the last chapter, might you challenge your community to embrace a season of consecration? Will you come before the Lord to pray with passion and persistence, contending for his will to be done in your life? You know God is ready to meet you. Will you and your community be willing to seek him? Take a step. Draw near to God. Seek him because he longs to be found.

GOD IS HERE, BUT WE DID NOT KNOW IT

God transformed my (Linson's) life in a lonely dorm room at the University of Texas at Austin. The great irony of this story is that most South Asian parents frowned upon sending their children to that "godless and dark city." They applauded the university for its academic excellence, but in their opinion, the great education was not worth the risk of losing one's faith.

But it was there, in that so-called dark place, in my own personal Babylon, that I experienced the greatest renewal of my life. The place that felt farthest away from God was the very place where God came to visit me. There is no place (and no person) that is too dark, too broken, or too sinful for the presence of God. If you patiently and prayerfully pay attention to his nudges, if you are willing to cry out to him, seek after him, and consecrate yourself, you will surely find him.

However, my story goes one step further.

That one encounter in my dorm room spread into a movement among my South Asian American friends on campus. I met others who longed for God, and we started seeking God together. My friends and I fasted and prayed every single Friday for two semesters. This discipline was clearly prompted and sustained by the Spirit; it was not our own strength. We prayed big prayers as we encountered God in deeper and more profound ways.

During these moments of encounter, we learned to trust and obey God. We took risks by sharing our faith with friends, starting new small group Bible studies, and praying for friends who were facing difficult situations. God intensified his calling and mission in our lives. Encountering God made us see our campus differently.

Over the next several years, God turned student after student back to him. I saw South Asian American students from all different types of worldviews give their lives to Christ. God was awakening many as he revived us. By the grace of God, what began as a group of friends seeking God at UT Austin has become a nationwide network—today there are groups like this meeting at universities all over the nation and creating a place for South Asian American students to encounter the living, triune God.

It all started in a place of isolation and cynicism. God met me right there and changed my life. Not just me, but hundreds of students across multiple decades until this very day. We were transformed and then sent in his presence.

It may be obvious, but I did not know God was going to do all this when I reached for my dad's Bible buried under the debris of the fall semester.

I felt like Jacob did as he was running away from his brother Esau. One night, after all that running, he lay on the ground and made a pillow from a nearby stone. As he fell asleep under the stars, he saw a dream of a ladder coming from heaven. The next morning he woke up and said, "The LORD is in this place, and I did not know it" (Geneses 28:16 ESV).

In the same way, my friends and I can testify that encountering God at the University of Texas at Austin was not what we expected or planned. God was the center of it all. He was there all along. But like Jacob, we did not know it . . . until we encountered him.

I believe the same can happen for you. God is here. Seek after him today.

4Es — **ENCOUNTER** — EXPLORE — EMPOWER — ESTABLISH

ENCOUNTER

God Is Moving

4

I (LINSON) REMEMBER HEARING A POWERFUL STORY about Bakht Singh, an evangelist and indigenous church planter from India. One of his partners recounts a moment they had on the beaches of Karachi, Pakistan:

> In Karachi, early one morning, Brother [Singh] said to me, "Let us go to pray together down on the seashore." I readily agreed, and off we went. Brother seemed to be no stranger to the area, and he took me straight to a stretch of beach that seemed to be more or less unknown to others, and we immediately knelt down in the sand.
>
> It was the cold season in Karachi, and to this day I remember how the warmth of the sand was very welcoming and comforting. Then Brother began to pray, sometimes in English and sometimes in Urdu. I found myself sharing deeply in his burden as he spread out the need of the whole area before God, and pleaded for a merciful entrance of God's light.
>
> Also, as the Holy Spirit moved him, he remembered, by name, those countless individuals who had asked him to pray for certain particular personal needs. His intercessions

were sometimes interspersed by pauses, and I had the sense that Brother was somehow "watching God," and listening for His responses.

I knelt alongside our Brother all through that day, occasionally praying to myself, and trying to express what was on my own heart at that time. It was, indeed, a day I shall never forget, and to God be the praise. All who know Brother will agree that this was typical of his whole "manner of life." Whatever were the pressures of the work, our Brother above all, longed to be close to his Lord.

I, myself, shall never be able to describe the "glow" and the "glory" that came upon us that day, as we knelt, hour after hour, in the sand. I only knew that I had been brought very near to God, for His work.[1]

We are struck by the way that Singh was *watching* God on the beaches of Karachi. It gives us the impression of a musician watching every flick and flutter of a conductor's baton or the way a wide receiver watches his quarterback's eyes and hands to ascertain the next play. It reminds us of the look one might receive from a spouse while visiting another household that explains everything without a single word—we see in his or her eyes that it is time to linger or to leave. There is a connection between people when they watch one another.

It is easy to assume that spirituality is static, and in many ways, that is true—silence, solitude, and stillness are often key ways to connect with God. But Singh suggests that there may be a deeper way of connecting with God that is dynamic because we are learning to watch his movements. Singh was ready to move if God moved. This might be a new idea to many of us, but our encounters with God will cause us to move. Why? Because God is not static. He is *motus Dei*—the God who moves.

GOD AS *MOTUS DEI*

What does it mean that God is moving? How does that impact our understanding of him?

The Father, the Son, and the Spirit move in cadence with one another as part of their existence. Though it is a bit hard to fathom, the Godhead moves toward each other in a mutually inhabiting, constantly infilling fashion as part of God's triune existence.[2] In a sense, God is moving toward God.

But God is also moving toward creation. Genesis 1 says the Spirit of God was moving—hovering over the waters. God the Father spoke forth his Word, which is the Son, and that Word moved toward the chaos and emptiness of the universe as it came into existence (Genesis 1:1-2). God was moving as part of his character, and from that intentional movement came the whole of the created order. Thus, not only does God move toward God, but God also moves toward creation.

To illustrate this idea further, God walked in the cool of the day in the garden with humanity (Genesis 3:8). God liberated his people from Egypt to lead them into the Promised Land (Exodus 1-12). He traveled with them as a pillar of cloud by day and fire by night (Exodus 13:22). His unique, tangible presence came down upon the transient tabernacle in the wilderness (Exodus 40:34). After the temple was built, God filled it with his *shekinah* (2 Chronicles 7:1). Then after the temple's destruction, God took a chariot, a wheel within a wheel, out of Jerusalem and into Babylon with the exiles (Ezekiel 1).

Unlike the gods and idols of the ancient Near East, Yahweh could move into new geographic locations without any interruption of power or sovereignty. He never abandoned his people but went with them, thus providing sanctuary in foreign lands.[3] He is the God of the entire heavens and the earth, not bound by territory or national political borders.

Even more marvelous than this, God the Son became flesh and tabernacled among us (John 1:1-14). God moved toward creation by becoming a human. Jesus Christ was both divine and human as he moved among us throughout the Judean countryside and local villages. Yes, Jesus was sent on mission—the *missio Dei* (i.e., mission of God), but undergirding that theological concept is that God is always moving in and through creation as *motus Dei*.

After Christ's ascension, we see glimpses of him again through the revelation that came to John at the isle of Patmos (Revelation 1:1-20). John sees Jesus Christ in his full glory preparing the church for his next move. Indeed, though the Spirit is already moving throughout the earth, Jesus Christ will also be returning to earth to bring history to its culmination. We have this current and coming blessed hope because God is moving toward us to reconcile all things unto himself (Ephesians 1:10).

Furthermore, as Christ moves throughout the earth in different times and places, he reveals himself in ways that humanity can find and understand him. Some scholars call this movement divine accommodation, which means that God moves to our level of understanding and comprehension.[4] For example, Christ may appear in dreams as more than a prophet as he moves toward some Muslims.[5] Or Christ may be revealed as the ultimate guru or sannyasi in which the entire world is his ashram, as he moves toward some Hindus.[6] Or consider how Christ moved toward some of the Sawi tribe of New Guinea, as he was revealed as the peace child offering.[7] Or Christ may be seen as a marginalized mestizo who brings liberty to the captives, as he moves toward some Latinos.[8] Not all will experience these specific moments, but overall God wants to reveal himself to humanity—he meets each of us. He moves toward us. This movement throughout the cultures of humanity is key to understanding God.

As *motus Dei*, God is moving toward himself, creation, and people of all cultures. This means God is not tamed or owned by any one people group, country, political party, or geography. No one can tame and master God. He is on the move. When we encounter him, it brings us great wonder and joy to join him as he subverts the cynicism of our day and expresses his reviving mission into new places all around us.

GOD MOVING IN AND AMONG HIS PEOPLE

Not only does God move, but God moves his people as they awaken to his reviving mission in the world. While there are many places in Scripture to see this, we will focus on three vignettes that exemplify this concept of movement: Moses at Mount Sinai, the disciples during Pentecost, and the revival in Samaria. In those narratives, we'll see that God is not static. Rather, he awakens and generates movement within his people toward his mission.

Moses encounters God at Mount Sinai. When God encounters Moses in Exodus 3, it is important to remember that it is God who moved the Hebrews into Egypt during the reign of Joseph. The psalmists tell the story as such: "And [God] sent a man before them—Joseph, sold as a slave" (Psalm 105:17).

As God talks with Moses from the burning bush, he describes his awareness of the plight of the Hebrews in Egypt and his proximity to their suffering using dynamic imagery. God heard their cries (v. 7). God states that "I have come down to rescue" (v. 8), which connotes that God is moving toward his people. After this powerful revelation that God is moving toward his people, Moses hears God say, "So now, go. I am sending you" (v. 10), which signifies that God is planning to move Moses as well.

However, God does not send Moses on a quest and then stay behind at Mount Sinai. Rather, God is going with Moses. God says, "I will be with you" (v. 12). Furthermore, God is already actively working in Egypt. God states, "I have watched over you [the Israelites] and have seen . . . " (v. 16), which shows that God is in motion among his people even amid their captivity. God continues by stating, "I have promised to bring you [the Israelites] . . . into the land" (v. 17), which illustrates that God is also going to go with them as they are liberated from Egypt into the Promised Land. Finally, God demonstrates his commitment to move with Moses and the people by promising, "When you have brought the people out of Egypt, you will worship God on this mountain" (v. 12).

Despite all these promises, Moses still feels unprepared and alone. So God says, "What about your brother, Aaron the Levite? I know he can speak well. He is already on his way to meet you" (Exodus 4:14), which shows that during his encounter with Moses, God had already started the process of moving Aaron toward his brother. Incredible. It fills me with wonder to see how God moves people as they encounter him. God is not far away, asking us to run errands for him, but rather, he is right there, moving with us and ahead of us.

Overall, we can see that God has a plan that requires his own movement and the movement of his people. But in the background, we sense that God is concerned not only for his people as a whole but also for these unique individuals. Because of his great love, concern, mercy, and grace, God is drawn toward us and goes with us to see his work come to fruition in and around us. As we encounter God, we must embrace that he is moving for our good and his glory.

The disciples encounter the Spirit in Jerusalem during Pentecost. Even before Pentecost in Acts 2, we can see the subtle hand of God moving people in and out of Jerusalem. Jewish communities had been dispersed and formed in new geographies (Mesopotamia, Cappadocia, Pontus, Asia, Egypt, Libya, Rome, etc.), but they had regathered in Jerusalem for the Pentecost festival. God set this scene into motion by moving people.[9]

Peter and the disciples experience a powerful movement of God, specifically the Holy Spirit moving down upon them: "They saw what seemed to be tongues of fire that separated and came to rest on each of them" (v. 3), which moves the disciples right into action. Peter "stood up" (v. 14) at the precipice of the upper room watching the Spirit working among the Jewish diaspora who had come from all over the world. Peter preaches a message referencing some obscure texts in the Scriptures (Joel 2:28-32 and Psalm 110:1) and masterfully ties them into the events currently unfolding in front of them with great conviction and coherence. No small feat for a fisherman!

Furthermore, the Spirit continues to spur the disciples into action as the mission front surges forward from Jerusalem into Judea, Samaria, and the uttermost parts of the earth. We see that as the disciples continue to encounter God, the migration of the people continues.

The disciples encounter the Spirit in Samaria and beyond. In Acts 8, we watch God continue to move the early church. Due to the persecution of this fledgling Christian community, the disciples are scattered further into new geographies (v. 1). God moves Philip into Samaria (v. 5). God moves Peter and John into Samaria (v. 14). God moves Philip southward to meet an Ethiopian, and God moves an Ethiopian to and from Jerusalem for a deeper encounter with himself (vv. 26-27). Finally, God moves Philip to another place supernaturally (v. 39). It is astounding to see that in this single chapter, the gospel goes from Jerusalem into the Judean countryside, then into Samaria, and then into the heart of an Ethiopian on his way to his homeland—a land that had to feel like the "ends of the earth" for the disciples. Furthermore, in Acts 11, after Stephen was martyred, the church scattered even further into

Antioch and these unnamed disciples spread the good news to Jews and Gentiles.

Seen through the lens of *motus Dei*, the book of Acts reads like an action novel. At every turn—from Jewish festivals to Samaritan villages to bustling cities—the Spirit is constantly on the initiative, awakening people to the everyday movement of God and catalyzing his reviving mission to the ends of the earth.

IN AWE OF A GOD WHO MOVES

God can move anywhere into any space. Clean, unclean, secular, sacred, professional, social, and everywhere in between. There is no place that is immune to the presence of God moving through his people. God transforms mundane places into holy places. Chariots, upper rooms, tanners' homes, and dining tables become sanctuaries as God moves into them.

This idea begins to untangle the cynicism being woven into various areas of our lives. Cynicism, like a dark winding rope, strangles our everyday circumstances of hope and goodwill. Amplified by the echo chambers of social media and news networks, it forms us into cynics among our coworkers, with our families, at our churches, and in our neighborhoods.

Sometimes we are caught unaware by the sinister belief that everyone is self-motivated, self-protective, and self-aggrandizing. We can start to believe that everything is a lie and pronounce judgment before we understand. This is not what God desires for us in these spaces and circumstances in life.

When God moves into our circumstances, and when God moves you and me into different spaces, wonder displaces cynicism. The contempt, apathy, selfishness, and cynicism in our world are not strong enough to keep God's movement at bay. Because of the Spirit of God that lives inside us, if God decides to move you and me into a geography, circumstance, or social space, that place will be different. The atmosphere and environment can change by the power of God within us. Consider how powerful and remarkable that is.

God has a plan to release his shalom, beauty, restoration, healing, and salvation in you, through you, all around you. Whether God is manifesting captivity and liberation for the Hebrews in Egypt, causing thousands of Jewish migrants at Pentecost to witness the Spirit's movement, prompting Philip to invite the salvation of a seeking Ethiopian official, or stirring you and me to take action in our particular localities, God is moving, and we get to move with him! No place in your city is off-limits to the presence of God. There is no corner of your campus or city where God isn't moving. And in your life, there is no limit to where God wants to move in and take up residence!

Our God can move anywhere. Are we willing to move with him?

PRACTICES TO ENCOUNTER GOD ON THE MOVE

How do these theological and scriptural concepts help us awaken to the movement of God? We need everyday, simple practices to help us awaken to God's presence and discern his movement all around us.

Like anything else, learning to discern the movement of God takes time and invites us into a balance. On the one hand, we should not let our anxiety and impatience rush us into action before we hear God's voice. On the other hand, we shouldn't become passive spectators, assuming God will do everything. God is moving, so we should be bold, but we must remember that it is God's initiative, not ours, so we should be humble. Bold humility is the mark of a person who has taken time to hone their discernment. We can embody that kind of bold humility through these concrete practices.

Embrace a growth mindset. As we see God moving, we must be willing to move with him, even if we're not totally sure what he's doing. Obedience is key. Even if we fail, we are growing and improving. When you sense a nudge from the Holy Spirit, just try it out and keep honing your discernment of God's voice, even if it feels awkward.[10] (We have to imagine that Philip felt more than a little awkward running next to an Ethiopian chariot, right?)

Thomas R. Kelly, in his book titled *A Testament of Devotion*, says it best: "Begin where you are. Obey now. Use what little obedience you are capable of, even if it be like a grain of mustard seed. Walk on the streets and chat with your friends. But every moment behind the scenes be in prayer, offering yourself in continuous obedience."[11] Some of my friends call this "playing the hunch"—if you believe that God is moving around you, take a step of faith and embrace a growth mindset, because some things are better experienced than explained.

Practice prayer walking. One of the best ways to experience the God who moves is to move while we experience God. Too often we assume that prayer needs to happen in isolated, quiet spaces with our eyes closed and our hands folded neatly in our laps. However, if God is moving, we can move with him and pray as we walk through our neighborhoods, campuses, and cities.

As you walk and pray, pay attention to your surroundings and notice if the Spirit is prompting you to pray for someone or something. For example, you might walk past a neighbor's house and be reminded to pray for a particular need in their family. Or you might walk by an elementary school and the Spirit might ask you to pray for teachers, children, and their well-being. Overall, moving while you pray helps you notice that God is moving all around you.

Sometimes we can ask God for a "clue" as to somewhere he wants us to go or someone he wants us to engage. Some people call this "treasure hunt" prayer walking because we're actively looking for the "treasure" God has told us about.

Though this might be a new practice for some, consider the Spirit's instructions to Philip in Acts 8, which we looked at above. The Spirit does not say, "Go south to the desert road where I want you to baptize an Ethiopian eunuch" (though that would have been significantly more straightforward!). Rather, the Spirit says, "Go south to the road—the desert road" (Acts 8:26), and only after Philip obeys that first "clue" does the Spirit say, "Go to that chariot and stay near it" (Acts 8:29).[12]

Let's unpack this prayer posture using a story as an illustration. A campus missionary in Texas asked her three students to pray for their campus. The students felt emboldened to go with God, meet others, and share the gospel; however, they did not know where to start. So they prayed.

One of the students felt that God was leading her to a nearby dorm, which was her own dorm—which felt logical. Another student said she felt like they should talk to a young man wearing a red jacket. The third student said she felt God telling her to go to the third floor. The young campus missionary was wildly impressed that all her students had heard something from God, so by embracing a growth mindset and practicing the discipline of prayer walking, she said, "Okay, let's go see what happens."

They walked over to the nearby dorm, went up to the third floor, and within moments a young man wearing a red lightweight track jacket came out of his dorm room. The students were stunned. This is the power of exploratory prayer! God is moving and wants you to join him as he moves. Like turning the steering wheel of a car when it's in park, discernment is more difficult when we are stagnant. It's as we embrace movement that we start to hone our discernment of God's invitations.

Facilitate divine encounters for others. God is not only encountering each of us; he wants you to encounter him too. Let's continue with our story. The three students stopped the young man with the red jacket and said, "Hey, this is going to sound weird, but we were praying and we kind of felt like we were supposed to run into you."

The young man was amazed. He went back into his dorm room and yelled at his suitemates, "You won't believe it! God just answered you."

The young man invited the students into the suite. Seated in the room were a bunch of guys talking about faith. One of them explained that a moment ago he had said something like, "If God was truly real, maybe he should give us some kind of sign."

In response, the young man with the red jacket told his friends he was frustrated by the conversation and was heading out to get some fresh air. That's when he ran into the prayer-walking students by the elevator.

Now everyone was stunned and filled with wonder. The three young students along with the campus missionary shared the gospel with those young men. They had many questions, so they decided to join a weekly Bible study in order to investigate God further. Simply amazing! Truly, the best thing we can offer anyone is an encounter with living God.

We're not saying this will happen every time—we've been on plenty of mundane prayer walks and played more than a few hunches that went nowhere—but this is the kind of thing that can happen when we follow the God who moves. As you encounter God, you learn that he loves people, wants to meet them, and is moving toward them. You get an opportunity to help facilitate that encounter, which cultivates wonder and awe in all of us.

Will you take a few moments to consider these steps in your life? Embrace a growth mindset by taking one small action out of your comfort zone on a regular basis. Engage in prayer walking—encountering God at work as you go about your regular life. God will speak to you. Look for an opportunity to facilitate a moment with God for others.

Strike up a conversation with a coworker who grabs your attention, or follow the Spirit's nudge by offering to pray with a friend who feels stuck or lost, or share the gospel with a friend who is seeking. Whatever it is, try it. God is moving you and others toward one another to encounter him.

GOD MOVES WITH THE KAREN PEOPLE

The Karen people are an ethnic group from Myanmar who, along with many other ethnic communities, have fled genocide in their country committed by the Burmese military. About ten years ago, a community of college students and their families began showing us firsthand how powerful it is to follow the God who moves and moves with his people. These students were a part of the first wave of Karen refugees to relocate to the United States.

As I (Eric) got to know the Karen students at the University of Nebraska at Omaha (UNO), they shared stories of fleeing with their families in the middle of the night as their villages burned. But when their communities ran for their lives, God went with them.

They settled into dense refugee camps in Thailand, some packed with fifty thousand people in less than a square mile. As they gathered in extended family groups in their temporary homes, they found that God was in their midst. He had moved with them.

When they left the refugee camps and were granted refugee status in the United States, they found themselves diving headfirst into culture shock (and climate shock!) as they settled into midwestern cities such as Omaha. The Karen students at UNO weren't ashamed of their refugee status. They were proud of their people's resilience and they fully embraced their new homes and communities.

As followers of Jesus they recognized another aspect of their identity. In the midst of the massive upheaval they had moved through, they weren't just refugees. They were sent ones. They saw themselves as moved by God to a new place and called to be a part of God's redemptive work wherever he moved them.

Within a semester of my getting to know a few Karen students, they decided to start a ministry on campus to create space for their friends to study the Bible in English and Karen. It quickly multiplied into several Bible studies as the Karen students connected with other refugee student groups. Soon a growing community of students from Somalia, South Sudan, Bhutan, and Myanmar were studying the Bible together.

It was a profoundly beautiful thing to study the story of Exodus with these refugee students. It wasn't theoretical for them. They had already experienced exodus firsthand. They knew the God who moves and moves with his people.

Around the same time we were helping resource these students to launch new ministries on campus, my wife and I attended a campus ministry conference in Poland with over 150 countries represented. While we were there, we met an incredible man from Myanmar. His life's calling was to travel around the world to any city where the diaspora of ethnic communities from Myanmar had spread. His message to them was simple yet powerful: "You are not just refugees. You are missionaries."

In refugee communities around the world he would encourage his people with the message that God had moved with them. He would challenge them to see themselves differently. Yes, it was evil that had caused their exodus. It was genocide, the evil actions of men. But God in his redemptive kindness had moved with them. In the midst of their movement, God was inviting them to join him in his mission to renew all things. They were moved not by choice, and not just by circumstances. They were moved by God, and God moved with them.

GOD UTILIZES DIASPORA AND *EKKLĒSIA*

The migration of people groups and the growing dispersion of ethnic groups throughout the globe are not mere coincidence. They are happening under the watchful care of God.

God scatters people to new places because we as humans embody his nature of movement. Sometimes this scattering of people happens due to legislation. For example, the Immigration and Nationality Act of 1965 eliminated racial and ethnic preferences for immigration to the United States. As a result, educated, English-speaking South Asians, among other Asian groups, came to the United States in droves looking for a better life. This scattering or dispersion of people is known as *diaspora*.

God's movement of people happens not only on a global scale but also on a local scale as he moves people like you and me to new places. For you, it might be a new job in a new city. It might be a new church community in a different part of town. It might be a new school district for your children. Instead of seeing these as difficulties to manage, what if we were to reinterpret these moves as orchestrated by the goodness of God and as opportunities to embody the characteristics of God? We are encountering a God who is moving us for our good and his glory. Along with seeing ourselves as a diaspora of ethnicity or nationality, we could imagine ourselves as a diaspora of the kingdom—scattered like seeds full of potential. With that frame of mind, an opportunity to embrace a lifestyle as his diaspora into new places emerges.

When we gather in these new places, we form an *ekklēsia*, which is the Greek word for a group of citizens called out from within a city to gather. This is also the word we translate as "church" in the

New Testament—even as we inhabit a location, we are the called-out ones of God. In that sense, diaspora and *ekklēsia* work together in this overall movement motif as intentional scattering and gathering of the people of God by the one who is *motus Dei*. It is the breathing in and out of the Holy Spirit of mission, the one who moves and moves people.

Amid this intentional scattering and gathering, we have an immense opportunity to encounter God in one place, then move with him to encounter him again with a group of others in that new place.

As we embrace this intentional movement, we decenter mission from its classical conception, which is as a movement emanating from a powerful center toward the margins. We experience more than a reverse mission, or the margins reaching back to the center. *Motus Dei* calls us deeper into a polycentric mission that takes us from every place to every place.

We embrace the call to be his diaspora and then become his *ekklēsia* again elsewhere, from place to place, people to people. We move with the winds of the Spirit of mission. In other words, our faith was made to travel.[13]

ENCOUNTER SUMMARY

The origin of reviving mission is encounter with God.

Who God is. Though our awareness can be dulled, the reality of God's presence is demonstrated by the ways he reveals himself as the God who is here. What's more, he is *motus Dei*—the God whose essence is marked by movement. As the God of *ekklēsia* and diaspora, he is the one who moves people in big and small ways to accomplish his purposes, and he is the God who is moving all around us today.

How we live. Encountering God's with-us-and-moving-around-us presence frees us from our cynicism and opens our lives to wonder. Because there is no place we can go where he is not already present and moving, we can embrace expectancy—watching God at work in the world around us.

What we do. We are invited to seek God through practices that help us awaken to his everyday movement in our ordinary lives—giving him our attention, offering him our consecration, pursuing him as we contend for breakthrough. What's more, we can grow in responding to his movement through embracing a growth mindset, practicing prayer walking, and looking for opportunities to facilitate divine encounter everywhere we go.

God's reviving mission isn't just about renewal in the world; it's about renewal in our lives as we experience a life wonder sourced in permanent encounter with God.

	WHO GOD IS	HOW WE LIVE	WHAT WE DO
ENCOUNTER God	God is here and God is moving.	Wonder versus cynicism	Seek God and respond to his movement.
EXPLORE what God is doing			
EMPOWER people			
ESTABLISH rhythms of community			

Figure 4.1. Reviving mission grid—encounter

4Es — ENCOUNTER — **EXPLORE** — EMPOWER — ESTABLISH

EXPLORE

Lift Up Your Eyes

CHIZU COULDN'T GET IMPERIAL VALLEY COLLEGE out of her head. Ever since she heard about this school out in the desert that didn't seem to be on any campus ministry's map, she couldn't stop thinking about it. Chizu was a campus minister living in San Diego. Should this isolated community college have been on her radar? Were campus ministers further to the north in Los Angeles thinking about Imperial Valley? Was anyone in Phoenix making the four-hour drive through the desert to Imperial Valley College?

These were the questions Chizu couldn't stop thinking about. Jesus was inviting her to lift her eyes and see how he was moving outside of her own natural sphere of concern.

One night Chizu was at a church prayer meeting when an older woman began to prophetically pray the words of Isaiah 43:19 over her:

> Behold, I am doing a new thing;
>   now it springs forth, do you not perceive it?
> I will make a way in the wilderness
>   and rivers in the desert. (ESV)

These words landed with surgical precision in just the place of Chizu's wrestling. God was moving. A new thing was springing up in the desert!

Chizu later described the effect of that prayer meeting: "I knew that she was talking about Imperial Valley College. I realized I had to go out there and pray. So I got my stuff, and I went. I kept thinking it was so crazy that I was going to drive two hours in the middle of the night just to pray! But I reminded myself that God had asked me to, and I knew I had to step through this door."

That night Chizu prayer walked the campus of Imperial Valley College. She walked the sidewalks, prayed over the buildings, and pictured the students who by that time had headed home to their families and their off-campus jobs. This place and these students were dearly loved by Jesus. And as Chizu allowed herself to be moved by God, her eyes were opened to see what God the Father was doing out in the desert.

After that spontaneous night of prayer, Chizu began a regular habit of making the long drive to pray at Imperial Valley College. Every time she prayed there, her conviction grew stronger that God was already present and moving on campus. She prayed that God would lead her to missional students who were actively seeking revival.

On her third visit, she met Elijah. Elijah was starting a new ministry on campus, and he quickly welcomed Chizu to come alongside him and his friends to encourage and support them as leaders. Soon a few of the students they met at Imperial Valley transferred to the nearby University of California extension campus, where they started another new community to help students encounter Jesus.

Chizu obeyed God's call to get in her car one night and drive two hours into the desert to a campus she knew almost nothing about. She saw that God was there, actively moving among students and stirring up longing for revival. Chizu's story shows us what it looks like to act on the fundamental assumption that God is here and God is moving.

ASSUME GOD IS MOVING

If God is present with us and if God is moving, then we can expect to find God at work everywhere we go. We can joyfully explore the activity of God all around us. In our neighborhoods, on our campuses, and in our churches, we don't need to ask the question, "*Is* God here?" or, "*Is* God doing anything?" Instead, we can declare with authority that God is present in this place and he is actively at work. We're free to ask the question, "*What* is God doing in this place?" That question is a game-changer. Over the next two chapters we'll invite you to wrestle with that question as we dig into the second *E*: Explore.

THE SECRET OF JESUS' MINISTRY

The assumption that God is present and moving was the secret at the center of Jesus' ministry. Jesus gives the secret away in John 5:19-20: "Truly, truly, I say to you, the Son can do nothing of his own accord, but only what he sees the Father doing. For whatever the Father does, that the Son does likewise. For the Father loves the Son and shows him all that he himself is doing" (ESV).

Think about the significance of what that means. Jesus, the incarnate image of God, the creative Word who formed the cosmos, could do nothing by himself. Every single thing he did was an act of seeing and recognizing the Father at work in the world and choosing to obediently join in with that work. Like Bakht Singh on the seashore of Karachi, Jesus was watching God. Every healing, every miracle, every act of compassion, every scathing rebuke to religious leaders, every prophetic word, every compelling sermon—all were acts of seeing and joining in with what he saw the Father doing. If God is here and God is moving, then, like Jesus, our job is to look with spiritual eyes, to ask the question, "What is God up to in this place?" and then to obediently join in.

To see how this principle played out in Jesus' life and ministry, let's look at two stories that bookend this revelation in John 5. There's a story in John 4 and a story in John 6 with each containing the repeated phrase "Lift up your eyes." This phrase is an Easter egg that instantly draws to mind a litany of stories in which prophets were invited to see not just the physical reality right in front of them, but a more real spiritual reality that God wanted to reveal. In the Hebrew Bible, variations of the phrase "Lift up your eyes" are repeated at least forty-six times. In at least thirty of those cases, this phrase is used when someone is lifting up their eyes to recognize something that's happening with spiritual significance, whether it's a supernatural vision (Daniel 10:5),[1] a moment of receiving a promise from God (Isaiah 60:4),[2] or recognition of a significant moment in the trajectory of one's life (Genesis 24:64).[3]

So when we see this same phrase in John's Gospel, it should bring all of this to mind. When Jesus lifts his eyes in John 4 and 6, he isn't just casually looking around; he's gazing at an unseen spiritual reality. And in light of Jesus' statement in John 5 that the Son can do only what he sees the Father doing, we can conclude that Jesus is lifting his eyes to see the activity of the Father in the world around him. Let's take a closer look.

JOHN 4: FIELDS RIPE FOR HARVEST OR AN INCONVENIENT DETOUR?

In John 4, when John writes that Jesus had to go through Samaria, there's a lot happening between the lines. Jesus was traveling from Jerusalem to Galilee, and in between was the region of Samaria. To get from Jerusalem to Galilee it was most convenient to walk through Samaria, but that's not what most Jewish religious leaders would do. Most would go out of their way to avoid Samaria at all costs. Jewish people did not consider Samaritans to be part of the people of God. They were seen as religious sellouts, people you shouldn't interact with.

So when we read that Jesus had to go through Samaria, we already know he's up to something intentional. When they arrived at a town called Sychar, Jesus' disciples went into town to buy food and Jesus struck up a life-changing conversation with a Samaritan woman who was drawing water from a well in the middle of the day.

When Jesus' disciples returned from buying food in the town, they saw Jesus talking with this woman, and it looked totally inappropriate to them. Jesus turned to his disciples and said, "Do you not say, 'There are yet four months, then comes the harvest'? Look, I tell you, lift up your eyes, and see that the fields are white for harvest" (John 4:35 ESV).

Not everyone saw the things Jesus saw. Jesus saw the Father at work in Samaria, so he intentionally went there and joined in. Jesus saw the Father actively at work in the life of a woman at a well. Jesus lifted his eyes and saw fields ripe for harvest. He saw a community of people desperate to encounter God and thirsty for living water. When Jesus lifted his eyes, he saw a season of spiritual receptivity that wasn't based on anything physically right in front of him. He saw the activity of God with spiritual eyes.

The disciples were looking at the same people as Jesus, but they did not see what Jesus saw. Jesus saw a woman with deep spiritual thirst who could bring the good news to her entire town. The disciples saw a woman they would never interact with or even acknowledge. Jesus saw fields bursting with harvest opportunity. The disciples saw a town full of Samaritans. They looked at Sychar and saw a place where God was not present and was not moving. They had the opposite of expectancy and curiosity. Their posture was apathy and contempt.

JOHN 6: AN OPPORTUNITY FOR ABUNDANCE OR AN UNWELCOME INTERRUPTION?

Similarly, just after Jesus' revelation in John 5, we find another "lift up your eyes" moment. John chapter 6 tells the story of Jesus getting away with his disciples to an isolated area, when a crowd of people descended on the place and interrupted Jesus' time with his followers. The text says that Jesus, "lifting up his eyes," saw the crowds, and turning to his disciples he said, "Where are we to buy bread, so that these people may eat?" (v. 5 ESV). In the next verse, John clues us in that Jesus already knew what he was about to do.

We can intuit from Jesus' words in John 5:19 that when he lifted up his eyes and saw the crowd coming toward him in John 6:5, he recognized his Father at work. He saw the Father preparing to display a miracle to feed a crowd of thousands. Jesus saw an opportunity to reveal something profound about his character—that he was the bread sent from heaven to satisfy our deepest spiritual hunger. In contrast to Jesus, the disciples were incredulous that Jesus would even ask such a ridiculous question—which reveals just how differently they were seeing the situation. They weren't seeing God at work, just the hungry faces of an imposing crowd.

Jesus saw a community of people hungry for God, hungry for something more. He saw his Father at work bringing these things to the surface, and he could see that God was present with power to do a miracle. The disciples looked at the same crowd, but instead of seeing spiritual hunger and an opportunity for a miracle, they saw a nuisance. They saw something that was taking away from their Jesus time. They saw an impossibility. Where Jesus saw supernatural abundance, they saw scarcity.

THE POSTURE OF CURIOSITY

What was it about Jesus' posture that enabled him to see what the disciples could not? Jesus knew that his Father was present and moving, so he was free to embrace a posture of expectancy and curiosity. Even in the "inconvenience" of a hungry crowd interrupting his time with his disciples, Jesus saw the Father at work. The question was not *if*, but *how*. Jesus was curious to see not *if* the Father was at work but *how* God was moving. Jesus embraced a posture of curiosity everywhere he went, asking, "Father, where are you at work? What are you doing in this person's life? How are you moving in this place?" And because he was curiously exploring the activity of the Father, he found it! In both stories, Jesus' posture was one of expectancy and curiosity.

So what was it about the disciples' posture that kept them from seeing as Jesus did? In both accounts, the disciples' posture was one of contempt. The disciples felt nothing but scorn for Samaritans and for the intrusive crowds. Their contempt cut them off from curiosity and from seeing what the Father was doing in these places and people. Contempt is the opposite of curiosity. Dr. John Gottman uses even stronger words: "Contempt is sulfuric acid for love."[4] Gottman is a psychologist who has become famous for being able to predict whether a couple will get divorced within just a few minutes of interacting with them. Malcolm Gladwell describes what Gottman is looking for in his bestselling book *Blink*: "If Gottman observes one or both partners in a marriage showing contempt toward the other, he considers it the most important sign that a marriage is in trouble."[5]

How often do we feel contempt for other people? Contempt for a person who interferes with our plans or the way we feel our lives should go? Contempt for people on the other side of an ideological divide? Contempt kills curiosity. If we look at other people with eyes of contempt, we will be blind to the work of God in their lives. If we feel contempt for a community or neighborhood, we will not find God at work there. But if we embrace a posture of curiosity, believing that God is already at work in people's lives, we can be free to care about them enough to learn their story. If we embrace a posture of genuine curiosity, we will be free to lift our eyes and awaken to the everyday movement of God around us.

SUPPORTING CAST MEMBERS OR MAIN CHARACTERS?

When we come into a place expecting to find God at work, it helps us see our place in the reviving mission of Jesus rightly. As we've shared, God is the main character in every story. When we follow the God who is already moving with a posture of expectancy and curiosity, we're free to see our role in the story clearly. In a supporting role, we can discern the invitation of God calling us to join in. This protects us against the harm we cause when we see ourselves as main characters or when we see our actions as the first and only expressions of Jesus' reviving mission in a place.

I (Eric) had an awkward conversation on an airplane several years ago. The person next to me struck up a conversation, and it turned out we were both involved in ministry. He was a white man who was planting a church in South Omaha, one of the largest Latino communities in Nebraska. When I asked him about his church and his vision for the community, he said, "Our church will be the first and only evangelical church in South Omaha!" I was taken aback because there's a church on almost every corner in that community. My wife (who's Mexican American) and I have experienced much hospitality and mentorship from incredible people of God there.

This guy didn't see any of that. It was clear that he saw himself and what he was doing as the only legitimate expression of Jesus' church in that place. His lack of awareness of the past and present faithfulness of God meant he risked locating himself and his church as the main characters in the story of South Omaha, and I feared for the harm his church would cause.

It's a dangerous thing to go into a place totally ignorant of the faithfulness of God for generations—to be ignorant of the history of generations of people who have loved God, who felt called to flee their countries and their homes, and to migrate across borders for the sake of their families. Communities of Latin American immigrants brought a resilient and deeply rooted faith in Jesus with them when they moved into these neighborhoods. This man couldn't see that God was already at work in the community through prophets and leaders and caregivers who know Jesus as the one who crosses borders with his people. It seemed that the only future he could imagine was his particular brand of church exalted over the community.

A THREE-ACT PLAY

Imagine with me that you are a supporting cast member in the second act of a three-act play. You've made it through act one. You and the audience know the story of what has happened so far. You know your lines and your role in the second act, and you also know where the story is going in act three. You know that you're a small (but essential!) part of a much bigger story, and this reality lets you play your part with joy and conviction.

Now, imagine what it would feel like to you as a cast member—and what it would feel like to the audience—if someone brand new walked on stage without any knowledge of acts one or three, without knowing any lines, and without even knowing that they were coming in midscene to an already unfolding story. Even worse, they think they're the main character in a story they really know nothing about. Imagine how ridiculous it would look for this person to make up lines and interpret the scene in front of them with only the limited context of what they could see. In that moment, they would completely derail the play and look like an absolute fool to the audience.

As sent ones, we must be aware of how God is already moving in a place, and that awareness should inform our role in the story. In every place we go, the activity of God precedes our presence. The activity of the Father, already at work, shapes our activity as we join in. And God's faithful presence in a place goes far beyond what we can see in the present moment.

Because God isn't just present in the present.

THE GOD WHO WAS, WHO IS, AND WHO IS TO COME

Scripture affirms again and again that our God is the one who was, who is, and who is to come (Revelation 1:4; 1:8; 4:8). Again, "Jesus Christ is the same yesterday and today and forever" (Hebrews 13:8). When Moses encountered God at the burning bush, God revealed himself to be faithfully present in Moses' past ("I am the God of your father," Exodus 3:6), in his present ("I have come down," Exodus 3:8), and in his future ("I will be with you," Exodus 3:12). God exists in the past, present, and future, so when we explore the activity of God in a place, our exploring likewise can be three-dimensional.

When you walk through your neighborhood, when you drive around your city, you can expect to find God at work in the moment because God is here and God is moving. But you can also be confident that the God who was and is and is to come has been at work in the past and will be at work in the future. You can explore the work of God in the past. You can be confident that in the history of that place, God has been faithful for generations. You can be assured that in the place God has called you, there is a future reality that God is building toward. God is actively working for the future redemption of all things.

Again, we look to Jesus as our example.

SYCHAR: A PLACE OF TEARING APART AND JOINING TOGETHER

Let's take another look at John 4 to see how Jesus' awareness of his Father's faithfulness in the past and future shaped his participation in the present.

Past. When Jesus walked into Sychar in Samaria, he was aware that this place was filled with history. As God incarnate, Jesus could remember the beautiful and painful moments that took place there. As Jesus looked around, he could see the legacy of his Father's faithfulness in that place. He could see Jacob's well. God had been faithful to Jacob, bringing him through family drama, conflict, and unreconciled relationships to put down roots in that place. Sychar was in the vicinity of an Old Testament city called Shechem. Many scholars even believe that Sychar and Shechem are two names for the same place.[6] It was in Shechem that Jacob settled down after reconciling with his brother Esau. God had been faithful to heal the deep wounds of division that existed between Esau and Jacob, and it was in this place that Jacob erected an altar of gratitude to God (Genesis 33:18-20). There was a legacy of faithfulness and reconciliation in the soil of Sychar.

Jesus could also remember a history of deep division with roots in Sychar. It was in Shechem that the kingdom of Israel was torn apart and descended into a two-hundred-year civil war as two divided nations (1 Kings 12). Jesus could see how division, hatred, and contempt had festered for centuries and how it had even affected the way his own disciples viewed towns like this.

Future. As Jesus looked around the town of Sychar, he could also see the future of abundant harvest he was building toward. Jesus knew that he would send out seventy-two of his followers to these same towns and that harvest truly was coming. Jesus could see that when the church was scattered from persecution in Acts 8, Philip and others would faithfully cross cultural divisions to go to the villages of Samaria with the gospel of Jesus. Churches would start in homes all throughout those communities. Jesus could see people filled with the Holy Spirit that would be poured out.

Jesus could see a future of reconciliation when he told the woman at the well that a time was coming when the divisions between Jerusalem (the Jewish center of worship) and Mount Gerizim (the center of worship for Samaritans) would be healed as people from diverse cultures worshiped God in spirit and truth (John 4:21-24). Jesus could look forward and see the spiritual fulfillment of prophecies spoken through Ezekiel and Jeremiah that people from the divided nations would be reconciled and would seek God in genuine worship together (Jeremiah 50:4-5; Ezekiel 37:16-22). And Jesus could see further still to a day when every tribe and nation would gather around the throne of God in worship (Revelation 7:9-12).

Present. Jesus walked into Sychar in the middle of the second act, but he knew his role as he watched his Father at work. He knew the events of act one that had shaped this place: events of violent division (the start of a civil war), of reconciliation (Jacob and Esau restored to relationship), and of the constant faithfulness of God. Jesus knew the grand conclusion of act three, that divided enemies would be reconciled and united in worship. And Jesus could see what his Father was doing right there in act two, saying, "The Father is seeking such people to worship him" (John 4:23 ESV). Jesus invited his disciples to lift their eyes and see what he already saw: that the fields of Sychar were ripe for harvest.

Jesus held all of this together (the history of violent division and collective contempt, the future of united worship, and the present of the Father seeking worshipers), and he played his part in the story beautifully. Jesus gazed at his Father, the one who was and is and is to come, and he joined in with what he saw his Father doing. As he did, Jesus ushered in revival in Sychar.

ALTAR TO AN UNKNOWN GOD IN ATHENS

The apostle Paul was also a master of exploring the movement of God in the past, present, and future. One of the best examples is found in Acts 17. Paul was alone in Athens waiting for Silas and Timothy to arrive from Berea, but he couldn't help exploring the city. It's not hard to imagine Paul exploring with spiritual eyes as he walked through Athens, searching for God at work in the present, looking for signs of his past faithfulness, and asking God what he would do in the future in this place. Like Jesus, Paul lifted his eyes to the spiritual reality of the city around him, and "his spirit was provoked within him as he saw that the city was full of idols" (v. 16 ESV). As he explored further, he found something interesting.

While Paul was observing the "objects of worship," he found an altar marked with this inscription: "TO AN UNKNOWN GOD" (v. 23). In a city full of idols to every god imaginable, what did it mean that there was an altar to an unknown God? Could it be that seeds of God's past faithfulness in Athens were planted right there in the soil of the land?

Third-century Greek historian Diogenes Laertius (who was not a Christian) recorded the history of how these altars to unknown gods came to be.[7] According to Diogenes, a plague broke out in the city around 595 BC. The Athenians tried sacrificing to every god they could think of, but nothing worked and the plague raged on. The Athenians consulted the oracle of Delphi, who instructed them to find the prophet Epimenides of Cnossos in Crete. They sent ships to Crete and found Epimenides, who agreed to return with them to purify their city.

Epimenides brought sheep into the Areopagus, the exact same open-air forum where Paul stood six hundred years later, and he released the sheep into the surrounding hills. He instructed the Athenian leaders to follow the sheep as they passed through the city and that if any sheep lay down without eating grass (an odd thing for a hungry sheep to do), they were to build an altar at that location and offer the sheep as a sacrifice to the unknown god.[8] Amazingly, many of the sheep lay down in grassy locations without eating. After the people built altars and sacrificed the sheep, the plague stopped. The Athenians were saved! To Epimenides they offered a talent of gold and a treaty of friendship between Cnossos and Athens. And they left the altars throughout their city as a reminder of the god they had never known but who had saved their city.

Look at how this history paints a richer and fuller picture of the faithfulness of God in that place. When Paul stepped into the Areopagus to speak, he opened his sermon by drawing these events to mind: "People of Athens! I see that in every way you are very religious. For as I walked around and looked carefully at your objects of worship, I even found an altar with this inscription: TO AN UNKNOWN GOD. So you are ignorant of the very thing you worship—and this is what I am going to proclaim to you" (Acts 17:22-23). This is profound! Paul stood in the exact place where Epimenides had introduced Athens to an unknown God six hundred years earlier, and remarkably, Paul even went on to quote Epimenides directly in his sermon to the Athenians, saying, "In him we live and move and have our being" (v. 28).[9]

Paul could have walked through Athens and taken this city of idols at face value. He could have limited his understanding to the physical things right in front of him. He could have assumed that his arrival marked the very first moment that God was revealed in Athens. He could have walked into the Areopagus and blasted them for their idolatry. Instead, he took a posture of curiosity, expecting to find God present and actively at work in the past, present, and future of Athens.[10] And what he discovered were monuments to God's past deliverance and testimonies about God's nearness from the mouths of their own prophets!

THREE-DIMENSIONAL EXPLORING

What does it look like in your city, in your neighborhood, or on your campus to explore with curiosity and spiritual vision to see the work of God in that place? How could you explore the place where Jesus has planted you with three-dimensional vision, to see the work of God in the past, present, and future as we follow the God who was and is and is to come? As Spirit-filled sent ones who are following Jesus into his reviving mission, we don't step into a place as the first people God has ever sent; we explore the presence of God already moving in the past, present, and future of that place.

EXPLORING IN THE PAST

As we explore the activity of God in the history of a place, we're looking for several things. Like Jesus in Sychar or Paul in Athens, we're expecting to find that God has been faithful in that place throughout history. We're looking for a generational legacy of the faithfulness of God.

When we explore how God has moved in the past, we're not just looking for a legacy of faithfulness and for seeds of the gospel. We also explore past wounds in the land, historic injustices, and generational brokenness. We expect to find past sin and hurts in need of present-day forgiveness and healing.

When Jesus stepped into the temple a week before his crucifixion, he called out religious leaders who didn't see their place in history accurately: "Woe to you, teachers of the law and Pharisees, you hypocrites! You build tombs for the prophets and decorate the graves of the righteous. And you say, 'If we had lived in the days of our ancestors, we would not have taken part with them in shedding the blood of the prophets'" (Matthew 23:29-30).

Jesus went on to recall specific instances of violence that were committed in the very site of the temple building they were standing in: "Therefore I am sending you prophets and sages and teachers. Some of them you will kill and crucify; others you will flog in your synagogues and pursue from town to town. And so upon you will come all the righteous blood that has been shed on earth, from the blood of righteous Abel to the blood of Zechariah son of Berekiah, whom you murdered between the temple and the altar" (Matthew 23:34-35).

When God confronted Cain for killing his brother Abel, God said, "Your brother's blood cries out to me from the ground" (Genesis 4:10). In Jesus' day and even now, there is blood in the soil. The blood of history cries out to God for justice.

We don't live in a vacuum. We live in places with history. God's people are called to acknowledge and learn the history of the places where he has sent us. And if we don't, the church will continue to be seen as irrelevant to this generation that's not satisfied with pretending everything is and always has been okay. The blood in the soil will not be satisfied with an erasure of history or with a sanitized version of history told by people unwilling to see their own story accurately. As a people, we will not see ourselves accurately if we cannot see and acknowledge our role in history. We will be unable to testify to the redeeming blood of Jesus, the same "sprinkled blood that speaks a better word than the blood of Abel" (Hebrews 12:24).

EXPLORING IN THE PRESENT

What does it look like in your community to explore the presence of God in the present? Take time to learn and celebrate what God is already doing, not just the new thing you want to do. Take time to prayer walk through your city, campus, or neighborhood and ask God to show you how he's moving.

One particular thing we're looking for as we explore the present is where the people of God are already investing. Cultivate partnership and not competition. We love this quote from Tim Webster, campus minister and member of the Oneida Nation: "When I treat ministry as my work, I can compete with other believers. When I seek to join God's work, I see others as colaborers."

EXPLORING IN THE FUTURE

As you explore the activity of the Father in a place, ask God to show you a future vision of what he is working toward. What does it look like to follow the God who is still to come in the place he has called you? Listen for the promises of God. Invite God to fill you with his Holy Spirit, the same Spirit he promised would reveal things that are yet to come (John 16:13). God's future promise of revival and redemption and justice should influence and shape the actions we're taking right now.

MEGAN'S STORY

A friend and mentor of ours had a powerful encounter with God as she looked painfully into the history of the place she was called to. Megan Krischke is a citizen of the Wyandotte Nation and is the national director of Native InterVarsity, a ministry that seeks to serve Native and Tribal students on campuses across the country. A few years ago, she was helping a group of Native students start a ministry on campus at Haskell Indian Nations University in Kansas, which before it was a university had been used as a boarding school where Native children were sent to be "educated" after they were forcibly removed from their families. Listen to the Holy Spirit with curiosity as you read this story in Megan's own words.

> As we prayed I saw the quad filled with the Native children from the era when the campus served as an Indian boarding school. The scene wasn't extraordinary; I just saw the children standing there in their school uniforms. But after that,

something unusual started happening: every time I closed my eyes to pray, I could see a young boy from that scene standing next to me and looking at me expectantly.

As I began sharing this situation with friends and seeking their thoughts, a wise young woman said to me, "Have you asked Jesus how he wants you to respond to the boy's presence?" I had not, but when I did, Jesus told me to take his hand and walk him home. So I returned to the image in prayer, took the boy's hand, and told him I was going to take him home. The final image that came to me in prayer was of the two of us walking hand in hand into the sun sitting on the horizon.

This experience showed me that Creator hasn't forgotten our painful histories—that not only our pain, but the pain and suffering of those who have already walked on, is close to his heart. He doesn't look at our pain and the pain of our ancestors and say, "That was a long time ago—you need to get over it." Instead, he invites us into a process of healing. He invites us to join him in setting things right in the present and in speaking his words of life and truth.

Following these times of prayer, Megan and the students she was coaching joined Jesus in his work of setting things right. They gathered a community of students on that campus to encounter the Jesus who saw their pain and invited them into healing.

Jesus invites us to embrace a posture of humble curiosity, lifting our eyes with expectancy. If we will respond to his invitation to explore with three-dimensional vision, we will find that God is powerfully at work in the present moment all around us, redeeming past wounds and working toward his promised future of making all things new.

4Es — ENCOUNTER — **EXPLORE** — EMPOWER — ESTABLISH

EXPLORE

People of Peace

6

ABOUT FIFTEEN YEARS AGO, my wife, Stacy, and I (Eric) uprooted our lives and made the long move from Southern California to Nebraska, following the voice of Jesus, who had clearly called us. At the time Nebraska was one of just three states in the country without any InterVarsity ministry, and we couldn't wait to get on campus and be a part of starting something new.

When we finally arrived at the University of Nebraska at Omaha (UNO), we were filled with hope for how God would move. We were in a constant state of exploring what God was doing there. We had heard several Scriptures from the Lord of how he was inviting us to join him in building a multiethnic community that would bring the love of God to every corner of campus. One corner of campus that we held a particular burden for was the growing community of Latino students.

We also had a lot of plans for how we would go about getting this new ministry started. We had ideas for how we could host outreach events, where we could start Bible studies, and what we would do to gather students to encounter Jesus. When we actually got to campus, we had to let most of those plans go. We found out we couldn't do anything in any official capacity on campus. We couldn't reserve rooms, we couldn't host official events, and we couldn't participate in official outreach activities.

We had done a lot of work to explore the place for what God was doing. We had learned history, met other ministry leaders, and clearly seen where Jesus was inviting us to join in the Father's work. Following Jesus' example of exploring the movement of God in a place usually means exploring the movement of God in people's lives. And as we threw all of our plans out the window at UNO, meeting people and finding out what God was doing in their lives was really all we had left.

What we found in that season of ministry was that God was already present and powerfully at work in people's lives. We saw it again and again.

We met Rene and Yanira, two Latino students who had just transferred to UNO that fall. When we shared the vision of starting a community where Latino students could grow in faith and in leadership, they both said that's exactly what they were looking for and they immediately started introducing us to their friends.

Yanira introduced us to Miguel, a freshman who told us how a señora in his church had recently shared a prophetic word that God would use him to start a new ministry on campus. As soon as he heard what we were up to, he made the connection and said, "I guess I'm supposed to help you start this!"

The pattern of meeting people who were right in the thick of wrestling with longing continued and expanded beyond Latino students. We met a young Black woman who was carrying a heavy burden for her community on campus. She had been praying that God would help her find a place for her and her friends to encounter Jesus and grow in their faith. She ended up starting a new group with us to do just that.

We met a Christian international student who was studying at UNO for just one semester along with four friends from her home university in China. She was curious about the Bible and asked for help starting a bilingual Bible study with her friends. It became a beautiful place of encounter with God. By the end of the semester all five of them ended up getting baptized!

This season fundamentally reshaped our understanding of mission as we saw vividly that God was already at work in people's lives. God was stoking spiritual hunger, cultivating longing, and inviting people to wrestle with their calling. It was a gift from God that we couldn't just reserve a space and start recruiting people like we had planned. It was life-giving to explore the activity of God in a place by searching for the spark of God's movement in the life of a person. Every week became a new adventure of exploring for spiritual treasure and finding people who were hungry for an encounter with God.

When we explore what God is doing, we do so not only in places but in people. Often what we're looking for in a place is in fact a person.

Let's look back at John 4 to see the ways that Jesus did this with the woman at the well.

JESUS SAW PEOPLE

When Jesus approached this woman, he truly saw her. He saw that she was drawing water alone at the hottest time of the day, when most women would go together as a community to draw water in the cooler times of the day. Looking purely at the physical reality before his eyes, Jesus could see that this woman was isolated and outcast. But Jesus saw much deeper than the physical. Just as he did with places, Jesus saw her story in three dimensions—past, present, and future.

Past: Jesus could see the series of broken relationships that she'd had with five previous husbands and the ways that pattern of dysfunction left her bound by shame and ostracized from her community.

Present: Jesus could see deeper, spiritual realities of her life in that moment. He could see her spiritual thirst—that she longed for something satisfying, something eternal. He could see that she was currently living with a man who was not her husband, that she was in a relationship that could not satisfy her. Jesus saw the spiritual longing in this woman's life for the Messiah.

Future: Jesus could look forward and see how God would pour out his Spirit on this woman and how rivers of living water would flow from her heart. Jesus could see a town desperate for the good news of God's anointed one, and he could see this woman being empowered with the gospel and sent as a missionary to her own community just moments later.

When Jesus looked at people, he expected to see the work of God in their lives. He knew he was stepping into a story that was already unfolding, so he was curious to learn their story, to know where they were coming from, and to see what God was up to.

As Jesus interacted with this woman, he listened for the words of his Father that would give her life. When she talked about the chore of getting water from the well every day, Jesus spoke words that addressed her deeper spiritual thirst. When she was comfortable to keep the conversation theoretical, hiding behind the differences between Jews and Samaritans, Jesus spoke words from God right to the heart of the matter. He said God desired more for her than worship in one location or another—God desired genuine worship from her at a spiritual level. When she expressed that one day the Messiah would reveal all things, Jesus revealed his identity in the clearest way he did to anyone in all of the gospel accounts. Nothing was veiled, nothing carried a hidden meaning; he spoke the words of God plainly and told her that he was the Messiah she longed for.

Jesus explored Sychar with a long-term vision of the movement of God in that place from the past to the present to the future. And that was the same way he explored the movement of God in this woman's life. He saw her whole story, from the broken past to the deeper spiritual needs of the moment, and he ultimately saw the promise God had for her life and the ways she would shape and impact her entire community.

PEOPLE OF PEACE

As we discussed in chapters three and four (encounter), we know that God is always present and always moving. Jesus never interacted with a person in whom God was not actively working. But sometimes Jesus recognized something more going on in the life of a person. Sometimes Jesus recognized a person who had been uniquely prepared by God to welcome Jesus with hospitality, to be especially open to his message, and to open up new networks for Jesus to impact more people's lives, just like the woman at the well. She was receptive to Jesus' message of soul satisfaction and living water. She didn't have strong relationships with her community, but that didn't stop her from going straight to her town, testifying of what God had done in her life. She responded with immediate action.

We see the same thing happen when Jesus met Levi at the tax booth in Mark 2. Levi was the definition of receptive. Jesus issued two words: "follow me." And Levi reoriented his whole life and left everything to follow him in that moment. Levi was hospitable to Jesus. Levi's first action as a follower of Jesus was to welcome Jesus into his home and host a party full of other tax collectors so that they could encounter the Jesus he had only just met.

Jesus gave a name to this pattern in Luke 10 when he sent out seventy-two of his followers. He told them that whenever they entered a house, they were to proclaim the peace of God over that place. They came with a message that the shalom of God had arrived, and if a person was receptive to that message, it was because they were themselves a person of peace. The home of a person of peace was to be ground zero for the kingdom of God breaking out in that town, and this pattern became one of the most essential missionary practices of the early church.

"I HAVE MANY IN THIS CITY WHO ARE MY PEOPLE"

One profound story that continues this "people of peace" pattern is found in Acts 18 in the city of Corinth. See if you can identify any common markers of a person of peace in the characters of this story.

When Paul arrived in Corinth, it was one of the few times when he was completely on his own. Being alone meant Paul had no community and no one to rely on for financial income, so, unlike in previous cities, he had to find a way to support himself. Paul had a background in leather work, but he couldn't just set up shop by himself. Most artisans such as leather workers would join a guild where they could share workspace, but in a pagan community a guild would be full of idol worship and sacrifice.

Thankfully, God in his goodness had people of peace waiting for Paul. Priscilla and her husband, Aquila, were part of the Jewish community that was deported from the city of Rome by the emperor Claudius following disruptions that emerged when the gospel arrived in Rome.[1] Priscilla and Aquila came with their family as refugees to Corinth, where they were able to practice their trade as leatherworkers.

They were probably part of a church community in Rome, but when they looked for a Christian community in Corinth, they found that it did not yet exist. When Paul arrived in Corinth, he was an answered prayer for them, just as they were an answered prayer for Paul. Priscilla and Aquila invited Paul to move in with them, to live in their home, to work in their communal workshop, and to depend on one another as a spiritual family. These were some of the closest friends Paul ever made. From day one, Priscilla and Aquila were people of hospitality. Even though they had experienced radical inhospitality at the hands of racist Roman policy, they continued to be people of hospitality. They couldn't help it! As people of peace, that's just how they were wired, so they welcomed Paul into community, and they grew with him as disciples of Jesus in Corinth.

In those days Paul would split his time between working with Priscilla and Aquila and sharing the gospel in Corinth. He began exploring for people of peace in one of his go-to starting spots: the synagogue. But he got only so far before the costs of division and conflict became too great and he was once again forced out, saying, "Your blood be on your own heads! I am innocent of it. From now on I will go to the Gentiles" (Acts 18:6).

Fortunately, once again, God had more people of peace in store. A Gentile named Titius Justus lived right next door to the synagogue, and he opened his home as a gathering place for the newly forming church. The synagogue ruler, Crispus, soon came to faith in Jesus and was baptized along with his entire household. But still Paul wondered if this city would follow the same pattern as every other. He wondered if his life would again be threatened and if he'd be forced to leave before he could stay long enough to really empower these people of peace God had brought him into relationship with.

On a particular night when Paul wrestled with his anxiety about what would happen next, Jesus came with a fresh encounter, proving again that God was present and moving. This encounter gave Paul supernatural comfort and clear instruction. "Do not be afraid," Jesus said. "Keep on speaking, do not be silent. For I am with you, and no one is going to attack and harm you, because I have many people in this city" (Acts 18:9-10).

The Greek word for "people" that Luke used to record this incident is *laos*. This is the same word used in the Septuagint, the Greek translation of the Old Testament, when God refers to his covenant people of Israel. Jesus promised Paul that there were many more people in Corinth who would be counted among the people of God. For Paul, the renewed task was clear: to explore for people of peace who would belong to Jesus.

After this encounter with Jesus, Paul doubled down on the call to explore for people of peace: people whose lives showed a spark of the movement of God. Paul remained eighteen months in the city of Corinth. It was the longest he had ever stayed in one city.

The pattern of exploring for people of peace is unmistakable throughout the Gospels and Acts. If we were to embrace this pattern in our ministries and churches, it would transform our experience of mission. We would begin to explore places, to look with spiritual eyes, and to awaken to the everyday movement of God. We would begin to see people as Jesus did, to learn their stories and hear about their past, their hurts, their dreams. We would ask God for prophetic vision, for the promises of God for people and for the Father's words to invite them into life. We would experience reviving mission in the way of Jesus!

RECOGNIZING PEOPLE OF PEACE

When we look for people of peace, what exactly are we looking for? Here's the pattern we notice again and again in the stories of Scripture: people of peace are receptive, relational, and responsive.

Receptive. People of peace are receptive and hospitable to the message and the messengers of Jesus. Priscilla and Aquila, Lydia, and the Philippian jailer all welcomed Paul into their homes and eagerly received the good news (Acts 16:15, 34; 18:3).

Relational. People of peace have relational networks that they open up for the gospel. When Cornelius, Crispus, and Stephanas came to faith in Jesus, their households and relational networks soon followed (Acts 10:48; 18:8; 1 Corinthians 1:16).

Responsive. People of peace respond by taking action. Within minutes of meeting Jesus, Levi threw a party and the Samaritan woman in Sychar started preaching to her town (Mark 2:14-15; John 4:28-30).

As you read about the traits of a person of peace, consider your own network. Is there anyone in your life who bears these same markers?

Who in your life who has been receptive to you? Who has shown spiritual curiosity? Who has asked questions about your spiritual life? We cannot miss that almost every person of peace mentioned in the narratives of Scripture offered food to the messenger. So who in your life has offered to have you over for dinner? Who in your workplace has taken you out to coffee? Who in your neighborhood has shared their family recipes with you? Aside from food, who has shown you emotional hospitality and relational warmth? We might miss the deeper thing going on if we don't recognize these as clear hallmarks of the supernatural work of God in a person's life.

Who do you know who is relational? As you seek to bring the kingdom of God close in your neighborhood, campus, or workplace, who do you know who has relational influence in that place? Who is at the center of the relational network there? If you are seeking to take on a particular cause in your city, who do you know who is networked with people who care about that same thing?

Who do you know who responds with action? Is there anyone in your life who always seems predisposed toward taking action? If you mention needs in your city or ideas you have, are there people in your life who consistently want to meet those needs or move those ideas into action?

If you know anyone who has these three markers, they are probably a person of peace. Knowing how to recognize people of peace is essential. But equally important is knowing how to go about finding people of peace, how to actively explore for people of peace in our neighborhoods and communities.

Remember, we're looking for a spark of the movement of God in the life of a person. And when we're exploring the work of God, our posture is curiosity. In the reviving mission of Jesus we can be sure that God is present and moving, so everywhere we go we look with curiosity, expecting to find God at work. Exploring for people of peace involves our posture as well as our practices. The next two sections will offer some suggested practices to help us embrace a posture of curiosity. We'll group these into two categories: being curious and provoking curiosity.

BEING CURIOUS

The word *curious* comes from the Latin root word *cura*, which means "to care." We love that! The invitation to be curious about people is fundamentally an invitation to care about them. When you care about someone, you want to know their story. You become invested in the things that matter to them. Jesus' posture of curiosity, his eager desire to see what God was doing in someone's life, was rooted in love for them. He was curious because he cared. Likewise, our curious exploration for people of peace should always be fueled by love.

Being curious is a hard thing to schedule into your week or to write into your ministry plan. It's got to be an all-the-time posture for how you relate to the people around you. Here are a few tips for embracing a posture of curiosity as you explore for a spark of the movement of God in people's lives.

Be curious about people's stories. This is basic, but it's a solid foundation for good evangelism and leadership development, and it's a strong place to start finding people of peace! Be curious to learn what's going on in people's lives. A little prophetic insight into people's past, like Jesus had with the woman at the well, can be helpful, but often this kind of insight is released by asking good questions and paying attention to what we see and hear. If there's a community where God has called you to be on mission (a neighborhood, a dorm, your workplace, a bar, etc.), get to know people in that place. Ask about their families. Ask about where they grew up. Ask what they love about their community and what they wish was different; find out where they see beauty and brokenness. Find out about their spiritual background. Have they had spiritual experiences that impacted their lives? Have they ever tried prayer? Have they had painful experiences with church or Christian communities?

Several years ago, I (Eric) spent a season directing a nonprofit organization focused on developing Christian leaders in the marketplace. I found that the big obstacle for Christians sharing their faith in their professional context wasn't a lack of strategy. People didn't usually need "three steps to have a spiritual conversation with your coworkers." It wasn't just that people weren't having spiritual conversations; they weren't having *any* kind of deeper conversations! What made the most impact was helping people choose to care enough about their coworkers to actually get to know the deeper things going on in their lives.

When we're genuinely curious, it's natural to learn about someone's family, about their hopes, dreams, and disappointments. It becomes natural to find out about their spiritual background and to be honest and vulnerable about our own spiritual journeys. It's possible to be more utilitarian in our search, looking for people of peace solely as a strategic step for ministry. But if that's our primary focus, then we're building on a foundation of using people, and that will never bear the kind of fruit that love can.

As you get to know people, you will have opportunities to ask good questions, and you should pay attention to what you hear, particularly the little nuggets that people drop in conversations. When a person shares something about their story, especially their spiritual journey, that's an opportunity to ask more questions and learn more about them. Listen to their words and stories with curious attention and at the same time listen and watch for what the Holy Spirit is saying or revealing. Ask the Holy Spirit to reveal the deeper hungers and thirsts in their life. Ask the Spirit to show you how Jesus is interceding with the Father for this person.

Be curious about networks. One key trait of people of peace is that they unlock relational networks. In his historical account of the early church, the biographer Luke was meticulous in his attention to relational networks, usually using the Greek word *oikos*, which means "house" or "household" but often carries a broader meaning of an extended relational network. A household of people in the first century did not refer to a mother, father, and 2.4 children. Several generations lived in one household, often with servants and extended family members living together.

Over a dozen times Luke mentions people's *oikos*, referring not to their physical home but to their network of relationships. When Cornelius was baptized, his whole *oikos* was baptized as well, and Luke spells out in Acts 10:24 that that included relatives and close friends. The same was true for Lydia (Acts 16:15), Crispus (Acts 18:8), Stephanas (1 Corinthians 1:16), and the Philippian jailer (Acts 16:32-34). You can quickly see the power of networks. In the book of Acts we see that the church didn't grow by the addition of individuals, it multiplied through entire communities bound together by social networks!

Having a posture of curiosity about networks was an essential lesson Stacy and I learned when we started a new ministry at the University of Nebraska at Omaha. As we met new students and got to know them, we shared the vision God had given us for "every corner of campus" and simply asked, "What's your corner of campus?" Often people of peace would reveal themselves right then and there, saying things like, "I'm on the baseball team and I wish we had a place for my teammates to experience the love of God." Or "I go to Alcoholics Anonymous meetings on campus, and I think I'm the only Christian there."

Sometimes people's relational networks aren't as obvious. One tool that can help you recognize and explore networks in your context is called network mapping. It's extremely simple, but network mapping has been a game-changer for each of us. Here are a few simple steps to create a network map for you or those you're working with:

1. Draw a small circle on a piece of paper and put your name in the middle.
2. From there, draw lines to other circles representing the different places where you spend time and have relationships. At this point, your name may be surrounded by circles like your neighborhood, your kids' school, your workplace, your favorite boba shop, your yoga class, a board game café, and so on.
3. Each of those circles represents a network of relationships, so your next step is to write the names of people you know in each of those places, and connect them with lines coming out of each circle. It might look something like figure 6.1.

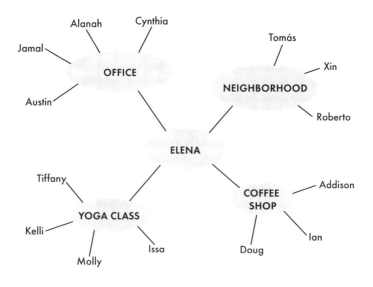

Figure 6.1. A network map

Explore: People of Peace

As you look at your network map, what do you notice about the people you're connected to? Are you connected to mostly other Christians? Mostly non-Christians? Are there any people of peace on your network map? Your network map isn't just a list of names. Each line represents a relationship between you and another person. How strong are those lines? Are there people you have a close, committed relationship with? Are there lines that are merely acquaintances? You probably have both and that's okay. Your job as a missionary is to grow and strengthen your network. That means adding more names as you get to know more people in the places where you do life and strengthening the relationships you have by getting to know people better.

Network mapping is great for an individual, but it's an even better tool for a community to do together. If you're in a small group, you could visualize your networks on one larger network map, paying attention to where your networks overlap. God may be highlighting a place to invest in mission as a community. As a church core team or campus fellowship you could create a network map of your whole community with different circles representing different "corners" of campus or neighborhoods and demographics of your city. Pay attention to where you've experienced the most breakthrough.

Paying attention to your networks as a community is a helpful embodiment of 1 Corinthians 12, that we're one body with many parts. Different ones of us will connect with different people and communities. None of us can reach everybody, but all of us can reach somebody. And that's the beauty of community, that in the diversity of our personalities and gifts and networks, we can do more together than any of us can do on our own.

PROVOKING CURIOSITY

Our own posture of curiosity is essential as we explore for people of peace. But we also rely on their curiosity. When we look at Jesus' ministry through the lens of the "people of peace" strategy, we start to see how much of his ministry was all about provoking curiosity and drawing people of peace to the surface. Jesus wasn't concerned with gathering a crowd. He had compassion on the crowds, but he knew they weren't all good soil. Like the sower in the parable in Mark 4, Jesus shared the word of God freely, but he was looking for people who would hear the word, accept it, and bear fruit thirty-, sixty-, and a hundredfold. Does that sound familiar? Jesus was looking for people of peace!

Jesus didn't just give out information for people to intellectually affirm or reject. He was intentionally provocative with his pointed questions, his miracles, and his parables. The purpose of the parables was to leave the crowds with a piece of the picture. Some were satisfied with that and went home. But others found their curiosity piqued, and they started wondering if there was more to the story. These people would go to Jesus for more. "When he was alone, the Twelve and the others around him asked him about the parables" (Mark 4:10). They would seek him out, follow him at any cost, and welcome him into their homes. Jesus lived in such a way that people's curiosity was provoked, and people of peace were constantly being drawn to the surface.

As we embrace a posture of curiosity about people, places, and networks, we are also challenged to live in such a way that people's curiosity is provoked. Here are some ways you can provoke curiosity in the lives of the people around you and draw out people of peace.

Share the gospel. The clearest way to find out if someone is a person of peace is by sharing the gospel and seeing how they respond. Yes, you will meet Christians in your context who will join you and open new networks as people of peace. But most people of peace in Scripture are people who had never heard the gospel. Lydia, the woman at the well, and the Philippian jailer all revealed themselves as people of peace by the way they responded to hearing the gospel. When they heard the good news, it provoked their curiosity and they showed receptivity, asking questions and ultimately responding with faith. If you want to find people of peace in your network, then share the gospel! Speak of Jesus and share the good news of what he's done in your life. Then pay attention and see whose curiosity is provoked.

Facilitate divine encounter. Everywhere we go and in everything we do, we facilitate opportunities for people to encounter Jesus. We are not purveyors of spiritual goods. We don't peddle ideas to spiritual consumers. We are facilitators of divine encounter, and we need to see ourselves as such. It is life-changing to recognize that the greatest gift we have to offer anyone (the *only* thing we have to offer anyone?) is an opportunity to encounter the living God.

One of the best ways to find people of peace is to help people encounter Jesus for themselves. When you help people encounter God, it becomes easy to recognize people of peace. If you lead a small group, a missional community, a microchurch, or any kind of Bible study, every gathering of your community is an opportunity to help people encounter God. Anytime a coworker, a gym buddy, or another parent from your kid's soccer team expresses a challenge they're facing or shows any kind of spiritual interest, that's an opportunity to help them encounter God. Offer to pray for them on the spot and see if God shows up.

One way we can facilitate divine encounter is to reveal the power of God through healing, miracles, and other kinds of signs. When someone experiences healing, that is a very powerful encounter with God. In planting contexts, healing can be a catalytic moment for a new faith community.

Of course, miracles don't always have this effect for everyone. When I was a junior in college, a football player on my dorm floor broke his foot and couldn't walk. He wasn't a Christian, but he was spiritually curious and one night he let me pray for Jesus to heal his foot. When he woke up the next morning his broken foot wasn't broken. The pain was entirely gone, and he could walk freely without crutches. He even checked with the athletic trainer and got permission to participate in practices.

When I asked him what he thought about the fact that Jesus miraculously healed his foot, his reaction was astounding. He shrugged and said, "Eh, sometimes things just happen. I'm not gonna overthink it." In the span of a few hours God had miraculously unbroken his foot, and he shrugged it off. If miracles and supernatural encounters with the power of God draw out people of peace, then the opposite is also true. Sometimes in response to signs from God, people reveal how closed off and unreceptive they really are.[2]

Testify and share stories. It's been said that one person's testimony is another person's prophecy. When we testify to what God is doing in our lives, we paint a prophetic picture for people to see what God could do in their lives too. Testimony draws people out to dream bigger dreams. It cultivates faith to imagine what could be possible. When we testify, we present our lives as living proof that God is present and active in the world, and when people hear stories of God's faithfulness, it infuses them with faith for what God could do for them. This is especially true of people of peace.

As you live a life of encounter with God, you will have countless stories of how God has shown up for you, convicted you, comforted you, and challenged you. God has entrusted you with experiences of his presence and stories of his deliverance. Don't bury those in the ground like the fearful servant in Jesus' parable of the talents (Matthew 25:14-30). Invest your stories and experiences of God's faithfulness into the lives of the people around you and watch where it bears fruit. People of peace will respond with curiosity. They'll ask more questions and show themselves to be spiritually receptive.

Sometimes the most powerful testimony we can share isn't a story of victory or breakthrough but a story of vulnerability. When I (Eric) was first planting a ministry among collegiate athletes, the group remained surface-level for about the first year. The community was growing, but everyone still wanted to look like they had it all together. Vulnerability felt like weakness.

Things started to change when my friend Maghan came to visit the campus. Maghan is a mentor of mine and she's a gifted prophet and planter. Like Jesus, she looked with spiritual eyes to see what the Father was doing in this young group of students. After just one meal with a few athletes, she prophesied to me, "This group is pretty shallow, but it will only take one person being vulnerable to crack the façade. That will happen soon, and it will change the environment of the whole athletic department."

Thank God for prophets! It was a helpful and timely word from God, and it foretold a breakthrough that happened almost immediately.

That night we hosted a gathering of student athletes to talk about human trafficking. At the end of the night we were all sitting in a circle and debriefing the event when a woman on the basketball team shocked everyone by sharing that she and her younger siblings spent several years living on the streets of San Francisco. She felt shaken by the human trafficking conversation because she recognized for the first time how vulnerable she and her siblings had really been. Her teammates, women who considered her one of their best friends, had no idea what she and her siblings had lived through. They wept as they looked around the room recognizing that they had no idea what was really going on in each other's lives. Just as Maghan had prophesied, that moment shattered the façade of everyone having it all together, and the images of perfection started falling like dominoes.

The next night a division one hockey player came to me in tears saying he hated the person he was becoming and despised the way he related to women. Another hockey player confided in a teammate that his parents were getting divorced, and he didn't know who to talk to about how sad he felt. Students started praying for each other every week. They became caring and curious about each other's lives, and people of peace started coming out of the woodwork! That semester a dozen student athletes started Bible studies on their teams, sometimes meeting in their locker rooms or on the bus to games. They had experienced the kingdom of God breaking through, they received it warmly, and they responded with action to create spaces for their teams—their *oikos*—to encounter Jesus too.

THE CASCADING EFFECT OF PEOPLE OF PEACE

Just before Miguel started his freshman year, he received a prophetic word that God would use him to start a new ministry on campus. That prophetic word bore incredible fruit during Miguel's college years. Like Levi and Lydia, as soon as Miguel caught the vision of God's kingdom coming close and Jesus ruling his life, he immediately turned toward his relational network to help his friends encounter the love of God too. He invested incarnationally in the multiethnic scholarship community he was a part of, connecting with several other people of peace who soon decided to follow Jesus themselves. He helped gather a community of Latino students that would launch several small groups, lead dozens of students to faith, and empower leaders who would go on to love and influence their communities and cities.

When Miguel graduated, he spent a few years working as a social worker and counselor, stewarding a call to care for the growing communities of Latin American immigrants in central Nebraska. He discipled young people in his church and encouraged them in their faith as they transitioned to college. This led him to connect with students at the University of Nebraska at Kearney (UNK), where he soon met another person of peace named Cesar. Cesar had recently decided to follow Jesus and was wrestling with a calling to reach his community of Latino students at UNK with the gospel.

Six years earlier, my wife and I had sat across the table from Miguel, a kind and talented seventeen-year-old, and affirmed God's calling on his life. Now Miguel got to sit across the table from Cesar as he wrestled with a similar calling. Miguel helped Cesar plant a Latino student ministry at UNK that soon grew into a network of ministries reaching athletes, international students, and fraternity and sorority students. A few years later, Miguel and Cesar helped plant a house church in a nearby town that created space for people to encounter Jesus, even if they had been hurt by the church.

When we first met Miguel, we had no idea that the word he'd received wasn't just a prophetic word for his first semester of college. It was actually the start of a lifelong calling to find people of peace and empower them to start new things on their campuses and in their communities. I'm sure that for the rest of his life, God will continue to bring people across Miguel's path who are wrestling with faith and discerning calling. This is how the mission of God revives people and communities, as people of peace are empowered to permeate their environments. This is the cascading power of people of peace.

EXPLORE SUMMARY

Reviving mission explores God's movement all around us. **Who God is.** Because God isn't just present in the present—he is the one who was and is and is to come—we are invited to respond to his movement in the past, present, and future of both the places we inhabit and the people we meet.

How we live. As we lift up our eyes to see the fullness of God's manifold work in places and among people we may not expect, we are challenged surrender our contempt and embrace curiosity. Like members of a supporting cast entering midway through a three-act play, we are delivered from the burden of being the main character. We are set free to embody curiosity wherever we go by asking the question, "God, what are you doing in this place?"

What we do. Like Jesus and those who followed him, we can learn to recognize God's three-dimensional work in the places we inhabit as we trace his past, present, and future work to make all things new. What's more, we can cooperate with his manifold work in our relational networks as we use curiosity to identify people of peace.

God's reviving mission invites us to explore for what he's already doing and play our part in the big story he's writing—a story that's good for us and good for the world!

	WHO GOD IS	HOW WE LIVE	WHAT WE DO
ENCOUNTER God	God is here and God is moving.	Wonder versus cynicism	Seek God and respond to his movement.
EXPLORE what God is doing	God is the one who was, is, and is to come.	Curiosity versus contempt	Recognize God's three-dimensional work in places and people.
EMPOWER people			
ESTABLISH rhythms of community			

Figure 6.2. Reviving mission grid—explore

4Es — ENCOUNTER — EXPLORE — **EMPOWER** — ESTABLISH

EMPOWER

By What Power?

7

AFTER THREE YEARS OF SEEING JESUS open blind eyes, heal paralyzed legs, and raise the dead, the people of Jerusalem surely had become accustomed to witnessing Jesus accomplish the impossible. Perhaps they viewed Jesus' miracles as the product of expertise—that Jesus was a prophet, a once-in-a-generation miracle worker. Maybe that's why it came as an even greater surprise when Jesus' followers started performing miracles, even after Jesus was gone.

Shortly after Jesus' death, Peter and John shocked the entire temple community by healing a forty-year-old man who hadn't walked in his entire life (Acts 3:1-10). The religious leaders recognized this as a powerful sign from God—the whole city saw it and went into a frenzy of "wonder and amazement." The community of priests and scribes had one question for these common, uneducated men who had walked with Jesus: "By what power or what name did you do this?" (Acts 4:7).

BY WHAT POWER?

Jesus' reviving mission was marked by supernatural power. His words, his actions, his miracles, his consistent practice of casting out demons—each of these demonstrated supernatural authority and left everyone asking some version of the same question: "By what power?"

When Jesus came to his hometown, preaching and teaching with authority and healing the sick, the crowds who heard him were dumbfounded. They asked, "How are such mighty works done by his hands?" (Mark 6:2 ESV).

Even king Herod had to wrestle with the question of who Jesus was and how he had such power. Herod wrongly concluded, "This is John the Baptist; he has risen from the dead! That is why miraculous powers are at work in him" (Matthew 14:2).

On one occasion, after seeing Jesus deliver a blind and mute man from demonic possession and restore his sight and speech, the crowds were again amazed and began to suggest the obvious interpretation: "Could this be the Son of David?" (Matthew 12:23). "Son of David" was a euphemism for the Messiah, God's anointed King who would usher in the eternal reign of God's kingdom. Pharisees in the same crowd saw Jesus work the same miracle, liberating a man from a kingdom of literal and spiritual darkness, but they offered a much more nefarious interpretation of where Jesus got his power: "It is only by Beelzebul, the prince of demons, that this fellow drives out demons" (Matthew 12:24).

In response Jesus gave away the secret to the source of his power, saying, "If Satan drives out Satan, he is divided against himself. How then can his kingdom stand? . . . But if it is by the Spirit of God that I drive out demons, then the kingdom of God has come upon you" (Matthew 12:26, 28).

For Jesus, the answer to the question, "By what power do you do these things?" is, undeniably, "By the power of the Holy Spirit."

HOLY SPIRIT POWER

Before Jesus ever preached a sermon, healed a person, or cast out a demon, he was baptized, the heavens were opened, and the Holy

Empower: By What Power?

Spirit descended upon him and filled him. After a period of testing and consecration in the wilderness, Jesus' launch into public ministry was described this way by Luke: "Jesus returned to Galilee in the power of the Spirit, and news about him spread through the whole countryside. He was teaching in their synagogues, and everyone praised him" (Luke 4:14-15).

Toward the end of his earthly ministry, Jesus promised his disciples they would be empowered in the very same way he was. In fact, he told them that if they believed in him, they would do the same works he did and even greater works, because he was going to the Father (John 14:12). That must have sounded unbelievable to the disciples in that moment. How could they possibly do greater works than Jesus?

Later that same night, Jesus said something even harder to believe. He told them it was for their good that he was going away; there was something even better for them than Jesus being physically present with them. He said, "It is for your good that I am going away. Unless I go away, the Advocate will not come to you; but if I go, I will send him to you" (John 16:7). What could be better than Jesus with them? Well, according to Jesus, the Holy Spirit.

Let that sink in. The Holy Spirit inside of you is better than Jesus next to you. Do you believe that? If Jesus could walk around with you and your friends each day and you could talk face-to-face about your decisions and activities, wouldn't that set you up for the best life imaginable? But Jesus said that it would be better for the living Spirit of God himself to fill your body and empower you to live a life of constant communion with him. Jesus facilitated encounter with God everywhere he went. The Holy Spirit enables us to live a life of permanent encounter. And when we live a life of permanent encounter with God, we live a life that is filled by, and becomes a channel for, the power of God.

That's why, after the resurrected Jesus appeared to his disciples for forty days, he charged them to not make a single move until they received the power of the Holy Spirit (also see Luke 24:49).

He ordered them not to depart from Jerusalem but to wait for the promise of the Father, which, he said, "you have heard me speak about. For John baptized with water, but in a few days you will be baptized with the Holy Spirit. . . . You will receive power when the Holy Spirit comes on you; and you will be my witnesses in Jerusalem, and in all Judea and Samaria, and to the ends of the earth" (Acts 1:4-5, 8).

And it happened just as Jesus said it would. They waited in Jerusalem to be clothed with power from on high, and at Pentecost the people of God were filled with the Holy Spirit of God. The story of Acts unfolds from there, with scene after scene of the power of God on full display before amazed and perplexed communities.

Peter and John healed a paralyzed man outside of the temple gate, and the onlooking religious leaders asked, "By what power or what name did you do this?" (Acts 4:7). A magician in Samaria watched men and women being filled with the Holy Spirit at the laying on of the apostles' hands, and he offered Peter money to receive the same power (Acts 9:9-19). Paul was twice mistaken for a god—once in Lystra (Acts 14:11) and once in Malta (Acts 28:6)—after displaying supernatural power for healing.

It wasn't always correctly interpreted, but the power of God was always on full display. And that power wasn't identified only with healing and miracles but with empowered lives and bold testimony as well: "With great power the apostles continued to testify to the resurrection of the Lord Jesus. And God's grace was so powerfully at work in them all" (Acts 4:33; also see 1 Corinthians 2:3-5; 1 Thessalonians 1:5; Romans 15:18-19).

The mission of the people of God has always been marked by the movement of the power of God. God is here. God is moving.

The God who is, was, and is to come is present and active in places and in people. The story of the reviving mission of God unfolding in the world is the story of God generously empowering his people with his own Spirit.

POWER IN ME

If Jesus' ministry and the ministry of his disciples was marked and defined by power, why are we uncomfortable with the idea of power in our own lives?

Many people pray to be healed. Fewer pray to be filled with the power of God to heal others. We say we believe in the power of God, and we even want to see the power of God. So why don't we want it to flow through us?

One of InterVarsity's student founders, Norman Grubb, described this same paradox more than eighty years ago in his book *Touching the Invisible*: "The inflow of almighty power into Christian lives is potentially ceaseless and can be taken for granted through grace; but what is rare and therefore necessary of emphasis is the faith that applies it. All believers say in a general way, 'God is Almighty,' 'God can do this or that.' Only one in a thousand says, 'God is almighty in me' and 'God will do so and so through me.'"[1]

How do you feel saying, "God is powerful in me!" or praying, "God, fill me with power!" If that makes you feel uncomfortable, you're not alone! It might be news to you that God wants to display his power in the world through people like you. This may be especially true if you come from a theological tradition that minimizes gifts of power and external expressions of the power of the Holy Spirit.

Even if we do embrace a theology of the power of God working in and flowing through God's people, we may still feel uncomfortable with this idea. Many of us shy away from the idea of "power in me" because of a misplaced sense of humility. It may feel inappropriate for us to desire power, even the power of God.

One of the biggest reasons many of us are uncomfortable with this is the numerous examples of counterfeit power in the world. We've seen the way power corrupts people. We've seen how the world deals with power as a zero-sum game, how people hold onto power with a scarcity mentality. History is filled with the stories of leaders who hoarded power at the expense of their people and ultimately to their own detriment. The world's posture toward power is one of narcissism: feeling entitled to power, hoarding power, and wielding power in the pursuit of our own interests.

Unfortunately, the church is no different. Stories of church leaders abusing power have become the norm. In response, many have come to believe that we should avoid power altogether. Our contention is that the solution to these counterfeit expressions of power is not the divesting of power but the multiplication of power.

While the world hoards power, God gives away power, and something amazing happens when he does. When God gives away power, it multiplies in and through the lives of his people. God's power empowers others! If there's one word we would use to capture God's posture toward power, it would be *generosity*. Through the Holy Spirit, the multiplying power of God has been generously given.

It's been said that "the best criticism of the bad is the practice of the better."[2] If we remain stuck in a posture of power avoidance, we are closing our hands to the gift of God and we will miss the opportunity to reveal something better to the counterfeit powers at play in our world. Our cities and neighborhoods are full of false powers. They don't need mission divested of power. They desperately need the power of God on full display. Let's look at the church in Ephesus to see what ministry without power looks like.

PICTURES OF POWERLESSNESS

The story of the church being planted in Ephesus is a story of the power of God breaking through in a city, a region, and the lives of individuals. At every stage there were dynamic power confrontations and constant conflict between the powers at play, both seen and unseen. In the midst of this story that unfolds in Acts 18 and 19, three vignettes paint an increasingly dire picture of what it looks like to lead without the power of the Holy Spirit.

Knowledge and passion without power: Apollos. Paul first arrived in Ephesus with two of his closest friends, Priscilla and Aquila, who remained in Ephesus while Paul took a trip back to Antioch and Jerusalem. One week, while Priscilla and Aquila were visiting the synagogue in Ephesus, they heard a Jewish man named Apollos preaching passionately about the Messiah who was to come. He was captivating to listen to. He spoke with eloquence and conviction. Priscilla and Aquila recognized God at work in this man, but they also noticed that something was off. Apollos didn't know the whole story!

Apollos was a disciple of John the Baptist who preached that the Messiah was coming soon. John the Baptist had invited the Jewish people to repent and be baptized in order to prepare themselves for the coming Christ. John made it clear that his baptism of repentance with water was a preview of the greater baptism coming in Jesus: "I baptize you with water for repentance. But after me comes one who is more powerful than I, whose sandals I am not worthy to carry. He will baptize you with the Holy Spirit and fire" (Matthew 3:11). Apollos had experienced the hope of coming revival! He was so passionate about this message that he was apparently traveling throughout the Roman Empire visiting communities of the Jewish diaspora and preaching John's gospel of hope and preparation. The problem was that he hadn't actually experienced it! He didn't know that it had already happened!

Apollos was a gifted communicator. He knew the right information about the Messiah who was to come. But he didn't know the presence or power of the Messiah. He didn't know the Holy Spirit in whom the Messiah baptized his people. When Priscilla and Aquila invited Apollos into their home and shared the whole story of Jesus, Apollos was empowered in a new way, and he soon set his vision even further than Ephesus, setting out to Corinth to preach the full gospel in the power of the Spirit.

Commitment and community without power: the twelve disciples of John. When Paul returned to Ephesus, he found even more disciples of John the Baptist. A community of twelve disciples of John had formed in Ephesus. It's unclear how so many disciples of John the Baptist ended up in Ephesus—they may have been involved in the same synagogue community where they heard the message of John the Baptist from Apollos. What's clear is that they had received John's message of baptism and had each made the decision to be baptized as an act of repentance and preparation for the Messiah. They formed a committed community and were trying to live out an active faith as a small subset of an already small religious minority in a city hostile to outside faiths.

Their experience of deep community, their commitment to one another, and their commitment to the message of John the Baptist were beautiful! But like Apollos, they didn't know the whole story. When Paul met with this community, he could tell they were missing something. His first question to them was, "Did you receive the Holy Spirit when you believed?" Not only had they not received the Holy Spirit, they had never even heard of the Holy Spirit! Paul shared that the Messiah had come in the person of Jesus, and after baptizing them in the name of Jesus, he laid his hands on each of them and prayed that they would be filled with the Holy Spirit. The Holy Spirit came on them and they immediately began manifesting signs of the powerful presence of

God, speaking in tongues and prophesying. They had their own personal Pentecost!

Strategy and technique without power: the seven sons of Sceva. If Apollos and the twelve disciples of John lacked the power of the Holy Spirit, then the next vignette reveals an even deeper deficit of power. As the community of Holy Spirit–filled believers continued to grow in Ephesus, the power of God was dramatically on display as people were healed of diseases and delivered from demonic oppression.

At this time a group of Jewish exorcists was traveling around trying to cast demons out of people; among them were the seven sons of a Jewish high priest named Sceva. Sceva's sons were amazed at Paul's power in setting people free from evil spirits. They knew that Paul rebuked demons in the name of Jesus and that it was incredibly effective, so they decided to try out this technique for themselves.

On one occasion they went to the home of a man who was possessed by a demon, and they tried using Paul's strategy of invoking the name of Jesus, saying, "In the name of the Jesus whom Paul preaches, I command you to come out" (Acts 19:13). The demon was not impressed by this technique. In a scene worthy of its own horror film, the evil spirit addressed the seven brothers, saying, "Jesus I know, and Paul I know about, but who are you?" (Acts 19:15).

The demonized man overpowered them all and sent them running away naked and wounded. The seven sons of Sceva had the right words and the right "tools" to cast out demons, but they had no power. They knew the name of Jesus, but they didn't know the Spirit of Jesus. They lacked the power of the Spirit that comes from intimacy with and obedience to Jesus.

TRUE EMPOWERMENT

Here's the problem: if we're honest, most of us would probably love having Apollos as a pastor. The twelve disciples of John in Ephesus look like a pretty healthy and committed small group. And though it's easy to see where the sons of Sceva fall short, if we're honest, we've all fallen short of empowerment when we've limited our focus to the right tools and talking points. That looks like pretty decent equipping. But none of these people were living or leading in the power of the Holy Spirit.

Empowerment can't mean just giving people the right tools and the right information. Empowerment is more than helping people find community, and it's more than charisma. Empowerment doesn't mean we hold all the power and dispense it to others at our discretion. True empowerment in the reviving mission of Jesus means helping people connect to the actual source of power: the Holy Spirit.

The spiritual stakes in Ephesus were too high for anything less than true empowerment. The story of the church in Ephesus is a story of the power of God at work in his people confronting the powers of darkness at work in the world, often with violent confrontations.

When the people of Ephesus witnessed the powerlessness of men trying to misuse the name of Jesus, they responded with fear and awe. Luke writes that in response to the failure of the sons of Sceva, "the name of the Lord Jesus was held in high honor" (Acts 19:17), and many people who tried to access power by practicing magic arts responded with repentance, even burning their books of sorcery. As the real power of God was displayed, people began to view illegitimate sources of power accurately. But not everyone welcomed this shift in power.

A silversmith named Demetrius convened a gathering of artisans who crafted and sold idols of the goddess Artemis, whose temple towered over the city. Apparently so many people were forsaking false sources of power that idol makers were going out of business! What a picture of revival!

Together the idol makers made a plan to turn the city against this new community of Christians using the powerful tool of nationalistic idolatry. They appealed to the regional pride and nationalism of the people of Ephesus, accusing Paul and the Christians of deposing the great goddess Artemis of her magnificence. When a man named Alexander got up to speak, the crowds recognized him as a Jew, and they became even more enraged. Luke records, "They all shouted in unison for about two hours: 'Great is Artemis of the Ephesians!'" (Acts 19:34). Whipping people into a fury of nationalistic idolatry is easy. Here we are two thousand years later and this is still a go-to strategy for leaders who want to wield and protect power for their own empire.

Do you see how the story of the church in Ephesus is a story of confronting powers? Look at all of the powers that were in opposition to the power of God in this story:

- Money has power. It was the power of God confronting the financial systems of Ephesus that led to the greatest opposition.
- Ethnic, regional, and national forms of pride have power. The appeal to "Make Artemis Great Again" instantaneously galvanized an entire city against the people of God.
- The crowd has power. It drew otherwise neutral people who had seen the power of God at work into choosing sides against the church.

In the story of Ephesus, we also see spiritual forces of darkness holding power in people's lives. Men and women were in bondage to evil spirits. An entire city worshiping the goddess Artemis for generations meant there was a spiritual stronghold of demonic power in the city.

These were not separate silos of power. Spiritual powers, social powers, financial powers, and others interplay to oppose the power of God. It's no wonder that when Paul wrote to these same communities of believers, he reminded them of the power of God at work within them that subdues and subverts every counterfeit source of power. Paul prayed that the Holy Spirit would empower them to know "his incomparably great power for us who believe. That power is the same as the mighty strength he exerted when he raised Christ from the dead and seated him at his right hand in the heavenly realms, far above all rule and authority, power and dominion, and every name that is invoked, not only in the present age but also in the one to come" (Ephesians 1:19-21).

HOW DO WE LIVE WITH MORE OF THE POWER OF GOD?

Like the believers in Ephesus, we are in desperate need of the power of God. We can't confront the idols of our land without it. We can't confront financial idols, deeply rooted racism and nationalistic idolatry, or the power of demonic oppression without the power of God. But in the face of these systemic powers and spiritual strongholds, we can be certain that God will always give us the power we need in order to do the things he has called us to do.

The power of God is generously given. The Holy Spirit of God himself lives inside our bodies. The ultimate creative power in the universe dwells within us. How much of the power of God we experience is not a question of God's willingness to give; it's a question of our capacity to receive.

Here we get to the heart of the issue of empowerment. If God is generous with his power, then the primary way we empower people is to help them receive what God is generously offering. So how do we do that?

In his book *Miracle Work*, Jordan Seng introduces a framework called the "power equation" that has profoundly shaped the way we think about power in our lives and what it means to empower people.[3] The essential idea is that while power is generously given by God, there are things we can do to strengthen our spiritual capacity to receive and operate in the power of God.

Seng beautifully applies this to supernatural ministries like healing, casting out demons, and prophesying, and if people aren't experiencing the power of God to heal and deliver in our ministries, we might not be fully operating in the power of the Holy Spirit. But at another level, we believe this framework applies to power for any kind of ministry. We long for more of the power of God in all of life—yes, power to heal and deliver, but also power to plant and preach. Power to care and serve. Power to neighbor and parent.

Here is Seng's framework of the power equation:

Authority + Gifting + Faith + Consecration = Power

Let's unpack this briefly.

Authority. Spiritual authority is all about intimacy with and obedience to Jesus. We operate in spiritual authority when we live our lives in the name of Jesus. The New Testament is full of examples of people living in Jesus' name: people heal, prophesy, and speak in the name of Jesus. This is a picture of people without their own authority operating in the authority of someone who commissioned them with some task. Servants don't have any authority of their own. But if a king sends a servant to do the king's business, then when that servant goes in the name of the king, they go with the king's authority and power, so long as they are actually about the king's business.

This is why Paul could cast out demons in the name of Jesus but the sons of Sceva could not. They were not living in intimacy with Jesus or in obedience to his word.

If you want to grow in authority, spend time growing intimately close with Jesus and choose to obey his words for you. If you want to empower someone, help them identify what the Holy Spirit is calling them to do and help them obey that calling.

Gifting. This may feel obvious, but when we minister out of the spiritual gifts God has given us, we minister with supernatural power. My (Eric's) wife, Stacy, is a gifted pastor (not vocationally, but in the biblical sense of the word), and the way she cares for and shepherds people is nothing short of supernatural. She works in higher education, and even though it's not in her job scope, students regularly come to her office to pour out the pain and anxiety they're experiencing in their lives.

Once when I was visiting her on campus, a student stormed into her office in tears. He had been working in the coffee shop across campus when he hit a breaking point of feeling overwhelmed and overworked. He walked out midshift and made a beeline for Stacy's office. In a moment of crisis he thought, "I can't take this anymore! But if I can just get to Stacy then everything will be okay." She cares for people so powerfully that anyone in need of care is drawn to her. We can all learn to become reasonably competent shepherds, but Stacy pastors with God-given power.

I (Eric) have an apostolic gifting, and I regularly have people come across my path who have a burden to start something new, to take on a particular injustice, or to invest incarnationally in a certain community. Often these people don't know where to start. Often they don't even feel like they have "permission" to start something new. I regularly get the privilege of sitting across the table (or computer screen) from someone and saying, "Yes! You can do that! You should start that thing!" When I'm operating in my apostolic gifting, God supernaturally delights to make connections to commission and send more people out into lives of mission.

This doesn't mean that only people with pastoral gifts should care for people, or only apostolic folks should start new things. We are all called to do evangelism, not just people with evangelistic gifts, and we're all called to pray for healing, not just those with healing gifts. But when we operate in our areas of gifting, we operate with supernatural power.

If you want to empower people in your church or on your campus, then work together to embrace the theological reality that you are part of one body with many other parts. Call out gifting in one another, release people to invest in their areas of gifting, and depend on one another for the gifts you don't have. We miss out on a lot of power by elevating one type of leadership as the model everyone should aspire to.

Faith. Jesus told his disciples, "If you believe, you will receive whatever you ask for in prayer" (Matthew 21:22). That may run contrary to our lived experience of prayer, but it's undeniable that, according to Jesus, faith is powerful. The Gospels are full of stories that draw a direct line between people's faith and their experience of the power of God. Jesus said the exact same phrase, "Your faith has made you well," to three different people in Luke's Gospel who had each just taken a bold risk based on a total assurance that Jesus had the power to heal (Luke 8:48; 17:19; 18:42; also see Acts 14:9-10).

If there are places in your life where it's hard to believe that God is present and working, spend time remembering past experiences of God's faithfulness to help cultivate faith in the present. Spend time in worship. When we remember who God is, our faith grows.

If you want to empower people in your community, invest in practices of cultivating faith together. Embrace a culture of testimony and celebration. Don't let an experience of God showing up for someone go by without testifying. Celebrate every win of God at work in people's lives. It wouldn't be an overstatement to say that one of our primary tasks in all of ministry is to increase people's faith. Every sermon, every Bible study, every conversation is an opportunity to help one another believe that God is present and actively at work in our lives and in the world around us. A community with faith like that is powerful.

Consecration. In chapter three we introduced consecration as an essential practice for encountering God's presence. It's also something that helps us depend on God's power. According to Seng, "Consecration refers to the way we dedicate ourselves to the things of God through specific sacrificial acts. The more of ourselves we set apart exclusively for God's use, the larger our capacity to flow in God's supernatural power."[4] Speaking about the biblical theme of setting things apart for God (setting the sabbath apart from everyday work, setting implements of temple worship apart from everyday use), he writes, "When things were set apart entirely for God, God could then use them with exceptional fullness."[5]

The same is true in our lives. The more of our lives that we sacrificially set apart for kingdom use, the more kingdom power we can experience. Notice that this is potentially related to acts of obedience and authority, but it's a little different. To increase our spiritual authority we surrender areas of disobedience in our lives (things like choosing to look at porn, getting drunk, or being selfish with money will lead us off our kingdom task as people sent by the king). For consecration we may choose to surrender something that's completely fine to have. We may choose to fast from food for a time, to give up coffee or access to certain technology, or to regularly invest in extended times of prayer. These acts of consecration are ways of saying, "God, I'm setting this thing aside because I want more of my life to be set aside for your kingdom."

One of the places we see the clear correlation between power and consecration is at the start of Jesus' ministry. When Jesus was led by the Holy Spirit into the wilderness for forty days of fasting, Luke wrote that Jesus was, "full of the Holy Spirit" (Luke 4:1). But after his forty days of fasting, "Jesus returned to Galilee in the *power* of the Spirit" (Luke 4:14, italics added). This was a time of intense consecration. (It was also a time of intentionally living in authority by obeying God in the face of temptation.)

In contrast, when Jesus' disciples lacked the power to cast a demon out of a young boy in Mark 9, he told them, "This kind can come out by nothing but prayer and fasting" (Mark 9:29 NKJV). We don't know what "this kind" means, but clearly fasting increases power. Jesus also pointed to a lack of faith in this interaction. Again, the variables of the equation always overlap.

MYSTERY AND STRATEGY

We hope you're seeing the connection between God's power, generously given, and our actions of cultivating and receiving that power. You could look at each variable in the power equation and object, "Only God gives that!" And you wouldn't be wrong. Jesus gave his disciples authority. God fills people with faith. God is the one who sets things and people apart as sacred. And God is the one who gives gifts. But we are called to cultivate these same things.

Living with God's power in our lives means both receiving what only God can give and choosing to strategically cultivate and apply it. James Choung and Ryan Pfeiffer, in their book *Longing for Revival*, provide helpful language to understand this paradox as a both/and of mystery and strategy.[6] The power of God is entirely mysterious. The Creator God of the universe delights to share his power with us. This is a profound mystery! But cultivating dependency on the power of God in our lives involves strategic habits and intentional choices.

Most of us very naturally default toward strategy *or* mystery. But the power equation gives us some simple ways to be strategic about increasing our access to the mysterious power of God in our lives. Do you want to live with greater spiritual authority? Then make choices to cultivate intimacy with and obedience to Jesus. Spend time in God's presence. Confess sin to a close friend. Take a few minutes to listen to the Holy Spirit right now and make a decision that you will obey whatever the Spirit says.

Do you want to increase your faith as a team before doing some kind of outreach activity or prayer ministry experience? Spend time testifying to one another and remember how God has shown up in power in the past. Watch how faith in God rises in the room. Do you want to grow in consecration? Consider setting apart more of your life for the purposes of the kingdom of God. Gather a few friends and try out fasting in community. It's all mystery; it's God's power filling and flowing through us. But it also involves strategy; we make intentional and wise decisions as a community to increase our access to the power of God.

ALEXIS AND LINDSEY'S STORY

Please note: the following story contains a brief description of a suicide attempt.

Alexis and Lindsey are two leaders who embody this kind of spiritual authority and power. These two Haitian American women are campus missionaries in Miami, and for the last few years they've been planting a ministry at an HBCU (Historically Black Colleges and Universities) where, from the start, stakes have been incredibly high. A few years ago a student died on campus and an administrator at the school reached out to local InterVarsity leaders, inviting them to invest in the spiritual lives of students on campus. This campus has been marked by tragedy after tragedy. There have been instances of suicide, violent deaths, and random accidents. It seems like every semester students are thrust into a state of mourning over friends they've lost.

One fall evening Alexis and Lindsey were attending a student-led Bible study on campus. Afterward Alexis was leading a time of prayer when the Holy Spirit prompted her to invite everyone in the room to pray against suicide on campus. Together they united in prayer, responding in obedience to the Holy Spirit's prompting. They prayed against the spirit of death that had robbed so much joy from students on campus. They prayed against suicide, that God would protect students from suicide and that suicide attempts on that campus would be unsuccessful. Specifically, Alexis had a sense from the Holy Spirit that someone was attempting suicide at that very moment.

When they finished praying, students began leaving the student center and heading back to their dorms. As one student approached his dorm, he heard the sound of sirens and an ambulance pulled up to the building he was approaching. EMTs ran into the building and down a hallway to the dorm room of a student who had just in that hour attempted to take his own life. The student was wheeled out on a stretcher and taken to the hospital where his life was saved. His suicide attempt was unsuccessful.

The student who witnessed this immediately ran back to the student center to tell everyone what had happened. The students' eyes were wide as they looked at each other and at Alexis and Lindsey. They were confronted with the same question as the temple community in Acts 4: What power is this? Some looked at Alexis like she had superpowers. Again, Alexis and Lindsey had the wisdom and spiritual vision to interpret the moment for their community.

"This is all Jesus," Alexis said. "This is what Jesus does. Jesus knows what's happening on this campus, and since we are his people, he makes us aware of what he's doing. Jesus is moving on this campus, and he's inviting us to join him."

That night in the student center, the power of God was on full display. God's power over darkness and death became real for a group of students who witnessed it firsthand. This is the reviving mission of Jesus.

To live a missional life means to live as an ambassador of King Jesus and to confront kingdoms and powers of darkness in our world. To live and lead like that, we desperately need the power of God. If we are sending people out from our churches and our campus ministries to lead on mission with Jesus, we had better be sure we are equipping them to lead with the power of God. There's too much on the line to merely give people tools and strategies. Sending people out with a couple of Bible study guides to confront a stronghold of death is like sending the sons of Sceva out with Paul's deliverance script and nothing else. If that's all we do, then our "empowerment" will leave people utterly unequipped to confront the darkness in our world. Alexis and Lindsey are living testimonies of the spiritual impact our lives can have if we will lead in the power of the Holy Spirit.

4Es — ENCOUNTER — EXPLORE — **EMPOWER** — ESTABLISH

8

EMPOWER

Serve and Send

CARMEN'S JOURNEY TOWARD starting the largest Black-owned business in Nebraska began with an encounter with God. As an executive in the call center industry, she looked around her city and couldn't help but recognize that people who looked like her had far fewer employment opportunities. In particular, when she looked at North Omaha, she saw that the employment rate was less than half that of the rest of the state. She held all of that before God, and she recognized that God was calling her to do something about it.

Her first impulse was to start a nonprofit focused on employment readiness, but as she prayed about that, God challenged her to do something different. "If you want to empower your community with jobs," she remembers God saying, "don't start a nonprofit; start a business."

So she took everything she knew about the call center industry and opened a call center in the heart of North Omaha.

Her mission from day one was not just to start a successful business, and it wasn't just to create jobs. Her mission was to empower people. A call center turned out to be an ideal model for what she wanted to do. She had decades of experience, the training on-ramp for working in a call center was extremely accessible, and the work itself created opportunities to impact the way her employees saw themselves.

A few months after starting North End Teleservices, Carmen invited a group of local industry executives to come to her facility and meet her employees. They didn't quite know what to do with what they saw. Most call centers invest a lot in training and on-ramping because they assume a high rate of turnover. They don't view call center jobs as careers; they assume everyone is on their way out. Because of that, they don't design workspaces around their employees' needs. They design the workspaces around efficiency, trying to fit the most people possible into a small space. Typically, that looks like rows of tiny desks with short divider walls separating employees by just a foot or two.

At North End Teleservices every employee has a large desk with drawers in their own cubicle and wall space to put up pictures of their families. When the other executives saw this, they were confused. They seemed most baffled by the drawers, asking questions like, "Why would they need drawers? What do they even put in them?"

It didn't matter what the employees put in their drawers; the drawers were there to make people feel like they had a career, not just a job. Pictures of family members on cubicle walls reminded them every day that they were in an environment built for them to thrive.

Carmen's business model is built on a holistic view of her team members' lives and well-being, and she constantly asks herself, "What do my employees need in order to thrive?" She let that question take her as far as she needed to go. One place it led her was to a local bank. She'd quickly learned that the majority of her employees didn't have bank accounts, so she started a partnership with a local bank to open checking and savings accounts for all of her employees. She brought in people to provide financial training, and she kept a deposit box in her office so employees could start saving money in the easiest way possible. When she learned that some of her employees lacked transportation, she bought two vans and began providing free rides to and from work for anyone who needed it.

Carmen currently employs over six hundred women and men in North Omaha, and she has given them much more than a job. She has empowered them through servanthood that honors who they are and addresses the tangible things they need to thrive holistically.

BUEY'S STORY: WITHOUT WATER, NOTHING CAN GROW

Buey's journey was very different from Carmen's, but it led him to a similar place of empowerment through serving. Buey was born in South Sudan, and one of his first experiences was walking across the desert with his mother to Ethiopia. Like most immigrant mothers, she was willing to give her son anything he needed in order to thrive. Their search for a place to thrive led them to Omaha, through a lot of culture shock, and into a community of Sudanese refugees. Through the sacrifices of his mother and community, Buey did thrive. He didn't even wait until he graduated from the University of Nebraska at Omaha to launch Aqua Africa (http://aqua-africa.net), an international nonprofit creating access to clean drinking water in South Sudan.

One of the common problems of NGOs going into Africa and "serving" people by digging wells in their towns is that they're often giving people something the people are not even asking for. Most NGOs do little to cultivate local investment in the well they're digging, and after they leave town, they often leave little infrastructure support behind to keep the well running. On average, most clean water wells put in place by foreign NGOs in Africa cease operating within two to three years. That's an incredible amount of financial investment with little sustainable impact.

Buey knew his people needed access to clean drinking water, but more than that, he wanted to empower them with ownership. Buey looked at his home country and asked the question, "What do my people need in order to thrive?" That question led him to a very different way of approaching clean water access in South Sudan. For one thing, Buey's team is majority South Sudanese, so from the start they're not coming in as outsiders. Also, Buey doesn't just look at a map and decide where he's putting a well next. He explores different communities and decides where to go based on where he is invited (essentially, he looks for people of peace!).

The wells have an incredible impact. For women who used to walk three miles a day to get water, having to walk only a few yards is literally life changing. As soon as a new well is operational, people start experiencing health breakthroughs from having clean drinking water. Headaches and stomachaches begin to disappear.

But the biggest difference in Buey's approach is that his primary investment in the community isn't a well; it's empowerment. Aqua Africa's motto is "Without water, nothing can grow," and while the visible "product" is a well, what truly grows and thrives is a strong local committee of women and men who are invested together in the work of running and operating their well and training others to do the same.

While the wells themselves take only three to four days to dig, Buey's teams stay in a village for one to two months mobilizing the community, coaching grassroots elections to empower the villages to elect a committee of local leaders, and training the committee to operate and maintain the well for themselves. While the average lifespan of a foreign-dug well in Sudan is two to three years, Aqua Africa's wells are going strong for ten plus years because Buey and his team are invested in serving the people in ways that empower them to holistically thrive.

APOSTOLIC SERVANTHOOD

Carmen and Buey are two of our heroes. They are living testimonies of the power of servanthood. Their lives and organizations are dynamic demonstrations of how whole communities can be empowered to thrive when women and men choose to live as servants.

In the reviving mission of Jesus we are sent as servants. We seek to empower the people around us with a posture of openhanded generosity, always asking the question, "What do these people need in order to thrive?" With a posture of generosity, we are free to serve and to send.

One way to describe this type of empowerment is the phrase "apostolic servanthood." Remember that our two English words *apostle* and *missionary* are rooted respectively in the Greek and Latin words *apostellō* and *missio,* which both mean "to send." Apostolic servanthood describes the nature of our sentness and the effect of our serving. We are sent to serve, and we serve to send.

Servanthood was central to Jesus' understanding of his mission and identity. Jesus defined his mission around servanthood, saying, "The Son of Man did not come to be served, but to serve" (Mark 10:45). This short statement reveals a profound paradox about servanthood and power. When Jesus refers to himself as "the Son of Man" he is bringing to mind this messianic image from Daniel 7:

> In my vision at night I looked, and there before me was one like a son of man, coming with the clouds of heaven. He approached the Ancient of Days and was led into his presence. He was given authority, glory and sovereign power; all nations and peoples of every language worshiped him.

His dominion is an everlasting dominion that will not pass away, and his kingdom is one that will never be destroyed. (Daniel 7:13-14)

This is a picture of the chosen one of God being given absolute power, authority, and dominion to rule and reign. It is a picture of complete power over the cosmos, and it's no small claim Jesus is making when he refers to himself this way. But what's even more mind-blowing is for Jesus to say that this Son of Man came not to be served but to serve.

For Jesus' followers, this picture of power and servanthood did not mix. If it was confounding for high-level business executives to see a CEO giving prime office space to call center workers, it was even more astounding for Jesus to speak of the Son of Man coming to serve. The all-powerful servant Messiah who rules the kingdom but serves his subjects did not fit in any of the preconceived boxes that existed in the minds of Jesus' followers.

What they had in mind was that Jesus would rule and be served, and as friends of Jesus they thought that they should be served as well! That's exactly what James and John were thinking when they asked the question that prompted this paradoxical response from Jesus.

In Mark 10:37, the brothers James and John made a bold request of Jesus: "Let one of us sit at your right and the other at your left in your glory." They probably had the Daniel 7 image of the Son of Man in mind. Jesus would sit on the throne with total authority, and all peoples and nations would serve him. James and John would sit on slightly smaller thrones to Jesus' right and left, and all nations would serve them too! Jesus was gracious in his response to their misguided request, but he didn't miss the chance to challenge his followers' fundamental misunderstanding of how power and servanthood worked in the kingdom of God.

Jesus first addressed the request itself. He told James and John they had absolutely no idea what they were asking. For them, sitting at the right and left of Jesus in his glory meant thrones of honor and power in Christ's eternal rule. For Jesus, it meant something entirely different. He said the places at his right and left were already prepared for someone else. The only other place in Mark's Gospel where the words "right and left" are used is at Jesus' crucifixion: "They crucified two rebels with him, one on his right and one on his left" (Mark 15:27).

Everything about Mark 10 points to the crucifixion. At this point in Jesus' ministry, he was within days of arriving in Jerusalem, where he knew he was going to die. Right before this interaction with James and John, Jesus had taken his disciples aside and told them that because they were going to Jerusalem, he would be killed.

Even the phrase "in your glory" meant something else to Jesus. Less than a week before his crucifixion, Jesus told his disciples, "The hour has come for the Son of Man to be glorified. Truly, truly, I say to you, unless a grain of wheat falls into the earth and dies, it remains alone; but if it dies, it bears much fruit" (John 12:23-24 ESV). Jesus in his glory is Jesus dying on a cross. The honor of sitting at Jesus' right and left in his glory was reserved for two unknown thieves. James and John truly had no idea what they were asking.

The other disciples were understandably frustrated with James and John for going behind their backs to ask for the best seats. In response, Jesus called them together around him and made the lesson about power and servanthood even more plain:

> You know that those who are regarded as rulers of the Gentiles lord it over them, and their high officials exercise authority over them. Not so with you. Instead, whoever wants to become great among you must be your servant, and whoever wants to be first must be slave of all. For even the

Son of Man did not come to be served, but to serve, and to give his life as a ransom for many. (Mark 10:42-45)

This is how power works in the world: the most powerful people relate to others by exercising authority and dominance over them. Even in many church contexts power means one person at the top who makes all of the decisions. Power means one person having undue authority in another person's life because of their position, rank, or gender. Again, this posture toward power is one of narcissism. In his book *When Narcissism Comes to Church*, Chuck DeGroat describes the model of narcissistic church leadership that far too many of us have witnessed:

> A narcissistic pastor cannot step away. In fact, in his mind he is essential in every decision. While he may speak of a vision that empowers the laity and staff, his actions say otherwise. Unlike the apostle Paul, who trained and commissioned others to travel, preach, and shepherd on his behalf, the narcissistic pastor cannot relinquish control. His hidden insecurity manifests in anxious, hypervigilant leadership in which significant meetings or decisions cannot happen without his blessing or presence. Often he arranges leadership structures and polity in such a way as to protect his authority at every level of decision-making.[1]

But the way of Jesus is exactly the opposite of these counterfeit pictures of power. Jesus is the King who serves. Jesus is the Son of Man, full of authority to rule, who lays down his life to serve the people he loves. Jesus full of glory and power is Jesus serving and sacrificing.

The Gospel writer John draws another strong connection between power and serving in the story of Jesus washing his disciples' feet:

> Jesus knew that the Father had put all things under his power, and that he had come from God and was returning to God; so he got up from the meal, took off his outer clothing, and wrapped a towel around his waist. After that, he poured water into a basin and began to wash his disciples' feet, drying them with the towel that was wrapped around him. (John 13:3-5)

Jesus knew that his Father had put all things under his power. And because Jesus was aware that all power was his, he lowered himself and served his friends, washing their feet. To his followers, especially Peter, it felt completely inappropriate for the person with the most power to be the one who served the most. But that is how power works in the kingdom of God.

It is precisely this theme that we see reflected in the final book of the Bible, the end of our story. In Revelation 5, John records a vision that again paints a picture of servanthood and power intertwined. In his vision John saw a scroll of the unfolding of time and history, and he wept bitterly because no one was found worthy to open the scroll. It seemed that no one was sovereign over the unfolding events of history. But then a herald of heaven said to John, "Do not weep! See, the Lion of the tribe of Judah . . . has triumphed. He is able to open the scroll" (Revelation 5:5). Here is a picture of power and strength. The lion who conquered! But wait. John turns to gaze at the glory of this conquering lion and what does he see? A *lamb*? And not just a lamb, a lamb looking like it had been slain. Here is the great conqueror who destroys death and liberates people living under the oppression of an unknown future: a slain lamb.

Again John saw the lamb enthroned:

> For the Lamb at the center of the throne
>   will be their shepherd;
> "he will lead them to springs of living water."

> "And God will wipe away every tear from their eyes."
> (Revelation 7:17)

At the throne of God, in the very power center of the universe, sits the embodiment of serving, sacrificial love: Jesus, the lamb who was slain.

What does Jesus do with power? Jesus serves.

What should we do with power? Serve.

Apostolic servanthood means we are sent to serve. In any context where we're trying to live missionally it is imperative that we see ourselves as servants. In places where we minister, we serve people.

Apostolic servanthood also means we serve to send. In places where we make an investment in people's lives, we serve with generosity and openhandedness, entrusting mission and autonomy to people who are the experts of their own context. As servants we remain fully ready to send people out into the places where Jesus is calling them to serve. We don't just recruit people out of their context and into our thing. We help them live as sent people in the places where Jesus has already planted them.

Let's look again at the church of Ephesus in Acts 18 and 19 to see the impact a community can have when it embraces the value of generous sending.

THE SERVING AND SENDING CHURCHES OF EPHESUS

The church network in Ephesus was marked by a generous embodiment of serving and sending from the start. Priscilla and Aquila took Apollos into their home to serve him by teaching him the way of Jesus and then they sent him to Corinth, recognizing what a gift he would be to the Corinthian church.

Priscilla and Aquila were empowered to steward their home as a place for spiritual extended family as they practiced the house-church model with Paul in Corinth. When they followed him to

Ephesus, they started a church in their home there, too. Paul confirmed this in his first letter to the church in Corinth, which he wrote from Ephesus, saying, "The churches in the province of Asia send you greetings. Aquila and Priscilla greet you warmly in the Lord, and so does the church that meets at their house" (1 Corinthians 16:19).

When Priscilla and Aquila were sent to Rome, they continued the pattern. When Paul wrote his letter to the churches in Rome he included this greeting to his dear friends: "Greet Priscilla and Aquila, my co-workers in Christ Jesus. They risked their lives for me. Not only I but all the churches of the Gentiles are grateful to them. Greet also the church that meets at their house" (Romans 16:3-5).

Apollos was sent to Corinth, Priscilla and Aquila were sent to Rome, and it seems there was a lot more sending than that. When Paul reached a breaking point with the synagogue, he withdrew with a community of disciples, and they began using the hall of Tyrannus as their primary place of formation and sending. Acts 19 doesn't give a lot of details, but we know that this community of disciples spent several hours each day together in the hall of Tyrannus and that Luke attributes this for the word being spread throughout the entire region of Asia Minor. Apparently, the hall of Tyrannus was a place of equipping and sending. Ephesus was a port city, so many residents of Asia Minor passed through and would have had opportunities to hear the word of the Lord. But the region of Asia Minor wasn't just coming to them. People were being sent out.

At some point in this two-year period a man named Epaphras heard the gospel in Ephesus and came to faith in Jesus. He was sent out as a missionary to his home city of Colossae, about a hundred miles inland from Ephesus. Epaphras planted churches in Colossae and nearby cities Hierapolis and Laodicea, where he served and empowered others to lead churches in their homes. A woman named Nympha led a church in her home in Laodicea. Philemon, Archippus, and Apphia led a church in their home in Colossae.

Look at the impact a culture of sending can make: Paul and this small community of believers invested in one place for a couple of years, and as people were sent out, they saw churches planted, supported, and sustained in at least five other cities!

The churches in Ephesus had such a strong culture of serving and sending that their entire region heard the good news of Jesus in the span of two years. As a community they embodied a beautiful posture of generosity and openhandedness. Even though sending out Apollos, Priscilla, Aquila, and Epaphras might have felt like a loss for their own community, their posture of generosity released them to be a blessing to Corinth, Rome, and Colossae.

Just as Jesus' posture toward power was one of generosity, the people of God are invited to take a generous posture of empowerment, serving and openhandedly blessing one another to go where Jesus calls.

INTEGRATED SERVING AND SENDING

When working to integrate two values simultaneously, we often find it helpful to represent them on a two-by-two grid (see fig. 8.1). When we visualize the values of serving and sending this way, we can see some of the ways we might fall short by emphasizing one of these values at the expense of the other, and what it looks like to genuinely integrate values of serving and sending at the same time. The y axis represents how well we're embodying a value for serving the people we want to empower. How are we serving them, supporting them, and making sure they have what they need to thrive? The x axis represents how well we're integrating the value of sending. How are we sending them, challenging them, and entrusting them with the mission? Look over figure 8.1. Maybe you can picture communities you've been a part of in some of these different quadrants.

Empower: Serve and Send

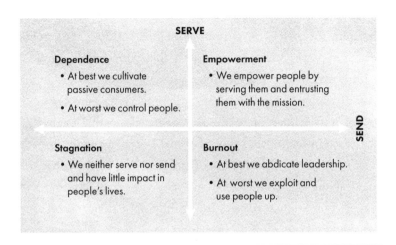

Figure 8.1. Serve and send grid

Serving but not sending: dependence. The upper left quadrant represents the sort of community we might have when we're serving but not sending. People are being served, invested in, and cared for in our ministry. But few challenges are given and little is asked of them. At best we're creating communities that are dependent on us, the kind of community where the "professionals" lead everything and people just come and consume. At worst we are maintaining a tight grip on control. We would label this quadrant as "dependence."

When I (Eric) think about this dependence quadrant, I'm reminded of my first semester of planting a ministry with student athletes at the University of Nebraska at Omaha. At the start of this ministry plant, I was so concerned about not asking too much of student athletes that I chose to do everything myself. In my desire to serve them, to provide spiritual leadership, to support them in the demands they were facing, I led everything. I left no room for challenge, no room to send them out as witnesses in their own context.

In this season no one was leading any ministries on their own teams. I hosted one gathering a week where I made dinner for twenty to thirty students, I led an inductive Bible study that was engaging for both Christian and non-Christian students, and I led a time of prayer ministry. I felt great about how excellently I was leading everything! The group was growing. Students were coming to faith in Jesus. Students from different teams were getting involved and several students even experienced supernatural healing!

I came to realize that this community was in the dependence quadrant when I asked some of the student athletes what they liked about this community and why they kept inviting their friends. One student named three things right away and everyone agreed. One: you cook us great food every week. Two: you teach the Bible well. Three: you're really funny.

Great. Each thing she named was something I did (by myself) and everyone else consumed. Everyone in the room came and consumed the food that I made, they consumed my teaching, and apparently my awkward unplanned jokes were landing with some success too. I had built a whole community around my own effort and my own personality. I had good intentions. I didn't want to burden students with leadership responsibilities when they were already so busy. But in the end, I was controlling everything. No one else was leading. No one else was having to wrestle with God each week to discern what to do next. And no one was taking any risks.

I could see we needed to shift to the right—toward real empowerment—by increasing our value for sending, but I wasn't sure how.

Sending but not serving: burnout. In the opposite corner of the grid, the lower right quadrant represents the kind of community we might have if we're sending but not serving. People are being challenged and sent out with missional responsibility. But they aren't being served or supported in significant ways to meet the challenges we're sending them into. We would label this quadrant as "burnout."

While I was planting an athlete community at UNO, I was also helping two people of peace start a new ministry at the University of Nebraska at Lincoln (UNL). Djenaba and Wylicia are two of the most amazing people of peace I've ever met. I connected with them at a citywide event we hosted with a local church to help students create communities for their friends to encounter Jesus. Djenaba and Wylicia were instantly responsive. They expressed a burden for their community: Black students at UNL.

At this time, there were only about five hundred Black students on this campus of over twenty-five thousand and they often experienced marginalization and racism. That year, Lincoln, Nebraska, came in at number seven on a national list of cities with the most anti-Black tweets per capita. The people sending those tweets were many of the same UNL students Djenaba and Wylicia sat next to in their classes and lived with in their dorms. The campus was an inhospitable environment for Black students, and Djenaba and Wylicia carried a calling from Jesus to create space for their friends to experience loving community and encounter Jesus.

One of the first things we did was to draw a network map, and in less than ten minutes they came up with over a hundred names of students they were connected with from different corners of campus: sororities and fraternities, athletic teams, dorms, the multicultural office, and anywhere else they set foot on campus.

They recognized Jesus calling them to start something new and they were willing to say yes. They embodied a high level of sentness! Once or twice a month I would make the drive to Lincoln and show up with food and try to support the work that they were doing, but they were leading everything. They reserved a space to host their weekly gathering, they invited all their friends, they led games and fun activities for students to get to know each other, and they would give short testimonies and facilitate discussions.

God was doing beautiful things in this new community on campus. Their community grew to about fifty students who gathered each week in a dorm lobby. One of the most beautiful things about their community was that over a third of the students involved weren't even Christian. At the end of the year, I met a freshman who said, "If it weren't for this group, I would have transferred. I'm still not sure about Jesus, but I need community like this."

In the midst of all the good things God was doing, I recognized that these student leaders were facing significant challenges and I wasn't giving them the support they needed to meet those challenges. I was the guy who showed up with snacks, but I can't say I was investing in their holistic well-being or discipling them very deeply. Again, my intentions were good. I didn't want to step in as a White guy and tell them how to reach their community. They were the experts of their own context, after all. But where I ended up was, at best, abdicating my role of serving and supporting them. At worst, I was using them to plant a ministry on a new campus without serving or equipping them to thrive. When challenges outpace support, people get burned out.

I could see that I needed to shift upward—toward real empowerment—by increasing the value for serving and supporting, but I wasn't sure how.

Serving and sending: empowering! The upper right quadrant is where genuine empowerment happens. When we integrate the values of serving and sending, we're building a culture of empowerment. In communities of empowerment the people we lead carry real leadership, they're entrusted with the mission, and they're sent to go where Jesus is calling them. At the same time, people are being served and supported. They're given the things they need in order to thrive holistically. They do face challenges, but those challenges are matched by the support they need to face them.

Carmen and Buey lead with this kind of empowerment. Carmen's employees don't just answer phones. Every time they take a call, they are challenged to see the human being on the other end of the line. They bring a nonanxious presence to stressed-out parents, and they offer care that can affect the lives of everyone who calls in. Carmen sets a high bar for her employees, but she serves them and supports them with the things they need to meet the challenges they face and to thrive holistically in every part of their lives. That is empowerment in the way of Jesus.

When many foreign NGOs show up to dig wells in South Sudanese villages, they are often "serving" people with something they haven't asked for and don't necessarily have the capacity to sustain. When Buey and his teams of South Sudanese women and men dig a well in a village, they empower communities with autonomy to select their own leaders and carry responsibility for their village's well-being together. They are served and sent! That is empowerment in the way of Jesus.

With athletes at UNO and Black students at UNL, I was missing the mark. But it wasn't too late! The Holy Spirit was faithful and present to convict me that the way I was leading was not empowerment. God invited me to do better. At UNO, we decided to start a core team of students who would carry leadership in the community and on their teams in particular. Different teams took turns bringing communal meals. Students began leading games and giving testimonies each week. Students took major risks to start Bible studies on their teams, removing barriers and putting the gospel as close as possible to the places where student athletes lived their lives. When we started a core team, it wasn't just me serving them; they were serving each other.

At UNL, we also started a core team. Inviting a few other students to lead meant Djenaba and Wylicia weren't leading on their own. During my campus visits I didn't try to connect with new students; the core team was already living and leading incarnationally on campus, growing and strengthening their own networks.

I was there to invest in the core team, to check in about life, to pray with them, and to help lead in the ways they actually wanted help. I served them by raising funds to help them bring their friends to conferences and retreats without a heavy financial burden. I also recognized that these students needed things I couldn't give. I invited them to some of InterVarsity's regional and national Black Campus Ministries (BCM) conferences and connected them to BCM leaders who could offer expert coaching and mentoring.

The answer to being in the dependence quadrant isn't to fully remove ourselves as leaders or to stop serving. The answer is to serve people toward sentness. We serve them with the best resource we have: an opportunity to encounter Jesus and to be filled with his Holy Spirit. We serve them by facilitating divine encounter, helping them recognize Jesus' loving invitation, and supporting them to step out in joyful obedience and faith-filled risk.

The answer to being in the burnout quadrant isn't to put ourselves in the middle of everything; it is to ask the question, "What do these people need in order to holistically thrive?" and then to serve and support them to live as joyful sent ones.

The Son of Man came not to be served, but to serve. Jesus came full of the power of God. What did he do with that power? He served. May we do likewise!

EMPOWER SUMMARY

Reviving mission depends on the empowerment of God.

Who God is. Just as Jesus and his earliest disciples were filled with power from on high, we too are invited to receive the fullness of God's person—the Holy Spirit given without measure. As hard as it might be to believe, the Holy Spirit inside of us is better than Jesus beside us, because the Spirit allows us to live a life of permanent encounter and enables us to empower others.

How we live. Recognizing the abundance of God invites us to become fundamentally generous people. We can subvert the narcissistic control that so often marks our culture's engagement with power with an embodied generosity that is quick to empower others into the dignity and calling God has given them.

What we do. Just as God has given to us, we give to others as we serve and send them in the power of the Holy Spirit. Though the empowerment of God is a mystery, we can strategically grow our capacity for God's empowerment through the "power equation." What's more, we can allow our leadership of others to be shaped not by unhealthy dependence or burnout, but by an integrative approach that enables them to experience the serving and sending power of God in their own lives.

The reviving mission of Jesus is fueled by the empowerment of God's Spirit given without measure and the people of God becoming like him in generosity.

	WHO GOD IS	HOW WE LIVE	WHAT WE DO
ENCOUNTER God	God is here and God is moving.	Wonder versus cynicism	Seek God and respond to his movement.
EXPLORE what God is doing	God is the one who was, is, and is to come.	Curiosity versus contempt	Recognize God's three-dimensional work in places and people.
EMPOWER people	God gives his Spirit without measure.	Generosity versus narcissism	Serve and send people in the power of the Holy Spirit.
ESTABLISH rhythms of community			

Figure 8.2. Reviving mission grid—empower

ESTABLISH

God of Cadence

IT WAS 2004. I (Linson) heard that familiar chime from my laptop and rushed to open the email application. I had been waiting several days for a reply to a specific email. Anticipation filled my heart when I saw the message sitting in my inbox. I clicked on it. The email opened. My heart fell.

I read the all too familiar refrain: "It was a pleasure to meet you and to learn more about your background and your interest in what we do. Unfortunately, we won't be offering you a position at this time. We were impressed by your interview and education, but we are pursuing another candidate who had more experience. Best of luck."

Crestfallen, I was not sure how I was going to tell my parents and brother that I did not get the job. It was my third or fourth rejection in the past few months.

Finally, I decided to call a close friend to share my story.

He suggested I stop striving and consider surrendering to God. I almost groaned aloud when I heard him launch into platitudes involving "being" before "doing." I'd never understood that concept and did not see how it applied to finding a job. In the end, he said something about fasting and praying.

For some reason, hearing about the spiritual discipline of fasting stopped me in my tracks. It did not occur to me that I should be fasting and praying for a potential job. But more than that, I felt God was calling me to meet him in a fresh way. Fasting was a familiar habit, but to consider it part of my job search felt new—I sensed God drawing near to me. I recognized the familiar pull of encounter.

Before I could say anything, my friend suggested we gather others, fast for forty days, and see what the Lord might do. I agreed. Within days, I had seven friends ready to fast and pray for various issues in our lives.

During the next forty days, we all fasted from meat, sweets, and fast food. Essentially, we ate fruits, vegetables, and grains. We also did not engage in social media and decided to spend sixty minutes every day in personal prayer and ninety minutes praying together each week. Spending this much time in an intentional communal spiritual rhythm was a major shift for me. But I was desperate for a breakthrough.

After just a few weeks, we felt refreshed and revived in our spirits. Our prayers felt powerful and effective. Scripture was alive and active. Our joy was grounded. The Holy Spirit was moving in our lives together. We enjoyed a sweet season of revival.

Even though I interviewed at a few more engineering firms during this fasting period, I did not find a job. Yet that did not deter my desire to spend time in this community. I didn't realize it fully at that time, but my friends and I were being transformed by God as we engaged in those habits individually and collectively.

Shortly after those forty days, we broke our fast together at a steakhouse, and we celebrated what God had done in our lives—we felt encouraged and resilient in our relationship with Jesus. But as I was driving home, I felt the Holy Spirit call me to go for another forty days of fasting and praying alone. It was that familiar pull of encounter . . . again.

Without even thinking, I agreed to follow the Spirit's guidance to continue my fasting and praying. It was much harder alone, but I persisted. I spent each night in prayer. I read through several chapters of the Bible and through key nonfiction books about prayer. I kept interviewing for jobs. I kept praying. I drew closer to Jesus. I felt the Spirit draw closer to me.

Around the conclusion of that second forty days, I received a phone call.

"We are pleased to offer you the role of project engineer. Your interview, education, and winsome attitude is just what we are looking for on our team. Can you start Monday?"

Dumbfounded, I said, "Yes!"

I was incredibly excited.

But amid that excitement, I felt the Spirit say I had received much more during these past eighty days than a new job. I knew that was true. Something had shifted within me. The habit of fasting and praying, both communally and individually, had shaped my life in a profound way.

Fun fact: after about five years of working as an engineer for various companies, God confirmed my call into full-time ministry. I resigned from the very engineering career I'd desperately desired for so long. After all, God gave me much more than a job. That season of fasting and prayer had been critical in my eventual decision to leave engineering. The experience created a cadence that shaped my understanding of God and provided me a habit I practice to this day.

Since that time, I have entered into many more individual and communal seasons of fasting, prayer, and consecration with great expectancy and hope. I've learned that our God is a God of cadence, and my habits help align my life with his timing.

THE POWER OF RIGHT HABITS

James Clear, author and speaker, states, "It is so easy to overestimate the importance of one defining moment and underestimate the value of making small improvements on a daily basis. Too often, we convince ourselves that massive results require massive action."[1] This is also true on a spiritual level.

Often we believe that God is going to change our lives, or the lives of people around us, in one incredible moment. It's true, that can happen, and it's happened to me. But often God is transforming our lives within the confines of our regular habits.

I am reminded of young David in the field watching over his father's sheep. He showed up every day, but in those moments alone, he wrote songs, he practiced using his sling, and he faced bears and lions. These were unnoticed habits that were being established in his private life, cultivating the resilient person he would become.

One day all those habits created a unique opportunity for him in a critical moment. He stepped up to face the Philistine champion, a giant named Goliath. His skill at using the sling was not supernaturally given to him, but it was honed because of his habits while protecting his father's sheep. His courage to face an adversary was not instantaneous, but it was forged because of his habit of facing predators of his father's flock. His desire to defend and honor the name of God was cultivated in his habits of worship and songwriting. David may be known as the champion who toppled a giant, but he was being formed into that person much earlier than this moment.

In the same way, we need to reconsider the importance we place on a single defining moment of transformation and recognize the ways God uses the daily habits of our lives to build our faith and form our next steps. Our lives and our communities need more than just a single moment—we need to establish habits in our lives.

Clear continues, "Improving by 1 percent isn't particularly notable, sometimes it isn't even *noticeable*—but it can be far more meaningful, especially in the long run. . . . It is only when looking back two, five, or perhaps ten years later that the value of good habits and the cost of bad ones becomes strikingly apparent."[2] The power of incremental change over time cannot be denied when we inspect our regular spiritual habits, and this is because our God isn't just a God of moments; he's a God of cadence, rhythms, and seasons.

As we've seen through previous chapters, the reviving mission of Jesus invites us to encounter his presence, explore his work among a people and place, and empower others with his Spirit. Yet the enduring power of the 4*E*s is the way they awaken us to the everyday movement of God. God's movement is found not in one moment of encounter, exploration, or empowerment but through establishing rhythms, disciplines, and habits that shape our individual and communal lives. It is as we embrace the cadence of God through our everyday habits that we begin to live with resilience—we live in sync with heaven.

GOD OF CADENCE, RHYTHM, AND SEASONS

Habits are essential to the reviving mission of Jesus because they are rooted in the person, creation, and wisdom of God. Just as the triune God has a cadence, so too does his creation have seasons, and there is great wisdom in aligning our lives with his rhythm.

Cadence in the person of God. In the doctrine of the Trinity, we come to understand that God's very essence is relational and God moves together in synchronicity. Father, Son, and Holy Spirit never overwhelm or overpower one another. Rather, in all humility, the persons of the Trinity make space for one another and move together in the rhythm of divine community.

Jesus said the Father and the Son are one (John 10:30) and in step with one another (John 17:21). Jesus also said the Spirit proceeds from the Father (John 14:26) and the Son (John 15:26) and the Spirit knows the very deep things of God (1 Corinthians 2:10-11), which illustrates this stunning triune rhythm. Essentially, the Godhead is at work together in divine unity and synchronicity. They have cadence.

Cadence in the creation of God. God designed order and rhythm into the cosmos, and it is because of this reality that our lives seem to thrive on the same kind of beautiful rhythm. God mandated that

> As long as the earth endures,
> seedtime and harvest,
> cold and heat,
> summer and winter,
> day and night
> will never cease. (Genesis 8:22)

Animals, plants, the elements, the starry host, the atoms of matter, children and parents, churches and communities—these all work together in cadence because that is the way it was created (Genesis 1:14).

Since we are made in the likeness of the triune God, we are his *imago Dei*, and because we inhabit a world of rhythm, humanity also craves and needs order, rhythm, cadence, and season to truly thrive. God's cadence is for our good and for the flourishing of others.

Cadence in the wisdom of God. The philosopher of Ecclesiastes states, "There is a time for everything, and a season for every activity under the heavens" (Ecclesiastes 3:1). Again, as the great statesman and prophet Daniel adds, it is God who

> changes times and seasons;
>> he deposes kings and raises up others.
> He gives wisdom to the wise
>> and knowledge to the discerning. (Daniel 2:21)

Jesus adds to this important understanding of heavenly timing by stating to his disciples, "It is not for you to know the times or dates the Father has set by his own authority" (Acts 1:7). Therefore, God implements a season and rhythm for everything and every affair—natural, political, and divine seasons are dictated by the wise involvement of God.

So what does this mean for us? We are in relationship with a God that has timing built into everything. There is rhythm to his work, and we can match that rhythm with our regular habits. Much like how a platoon sergeant calls forth the marching cadence, we are invited to set our lives to the beat of God's drum, not ours. We get the opportunity to embrace and establish habits that form us into the people God created us to be.

As a person engaged in the marketplace, how can you practice specific habits every day that allow the presence of God to consecrate that space? As a stay-at-home parent, how would you embody simple habits that bring your children and family closer to the Lord? As a college student, could you practice habits of gathering people together regularly and see how the Spirit moves among you?

Consider establishing new habits in your daily life. No matter how mundane we think they are, habits such as regularly praying, fasting, and gathering are key to opening us up to what God is doing in our community for that season and moment. We have the important task of not only being edified ourselves through habits but inviting others into these practices to be formed into his likeness together.

KAIROS AND OUR REGULAR HABITS

To take this idea further, the writers of the New Testament used two different Greek words to describe elements of time: *chronos* and *kairos*. Habits take up our time every day, but we believe that God is using that time in key ways.

The first word, *chronos*, from which we get the word *chronological*, is defined simply as a passage of time, a space of time, or a typical season.[3] Our habits occupy *chronos* every single day, and sometimes the passing of *chronos* becomes boring or mundane. *Chronos* is the word used in Acts 27:9: "Much time had been lost, and sailing had already become dangerous." The predictable progression of days and weeks meant the season had changed.

Kairos on the other hand is defined as an appointed season, a due time, or a proper occasion or moment of a matter.[4] Leonard Ravenhill, evangelist and author, loosely defines *kairos* as "the opportunity of a lifetime, which must be seized within the lifetime of that opportunity."[5] This means there are moments in which we see incredible breakthroughs in a person or a community that feel ordained by heaven. *Kairos* is the word used in Mark 1:15: "The time is fulfilled, and the kingdom of God is at hand; repent and believe in the gospel" (ESV). The time being fulfilled isn't about a certain day on the calendar. It's the moment of heaven-ordained breakthrough as Jesus steps out to proclaim that the kingdom has drawn near.

When we bring these two concepts of time together, we can see the deep power of establishing habits. Our habits practiced within the everyday rhythms of *chronos* help us awaken to the opportune moments of *kairos* being initiated by God. Said differently, we are prone to miss opportunities (*kairos*) because we have not established daily (*chronos*) habits. Imagine what we are overlooking by not establishing spiritual habits for ourselves or our community.

Since we cannot predict or conjure the timing of God, we practice our habits regularly. In that way our habits really matter. If we are not made malleable by these habits in *chronos*, we can fail to recognize those *kairos* moments when they suddenly happen around us; essentially, we can become out of sync with the God of cadence!

We do not want you to miss an important moment for you, your family, or your community simply because your habits have grown stale, weak, unfruitful, or even nonexistent. How tragic that would be for each of us! This is the double beauty in establishing habits: first, our habits help us transform into the likeness of Christ, but second, these habits also build our sensitivity to key opportunities. Over time, this creates resilience in our daily discipleship.

HABITS OF THE EARLY CHURCH

We know we need to be in sync with the God of cadence, so the question becomes, which habits help us awaken to the everyday movement of God and participate in his reviving mission?

Throughout the book of Acts, Paul traveled back to visit fledgling Christian communities, "strengthening the disciples and encouraging them to remain true to the faith" (Acts 14:22). How did Paul strengthen and encourage them? He established habits.

We believe that Paul knew he could not lead this growing movement alone. He knew he was not the center of it. Instead, each church had to lock into what God was doing among them by establishing key habits. Each church had to understand God's cadence and timing for their community and move in sync and in season with the Holy Spirit.

So how did Paul cultivate that sensitivity in the churches he was planting? Again, he taught them spiritual habits that were rooted in the life of Jesus. Essentially, we see the pattern in the ministry of Jesus and then deployed contextually in the ministry of Paul. Let's unpack these groups of habits.

Habits of encounter: fasting and prayer. First, Paul established habits of encounter through fasting and praying (Acts 14:23). Jesus, as the archetype for Paul, taught in the Sermon on the Mount that *when* his followers fasted (not *if*), they should not make a scene or curate a righteous, pretentious piety in front of others. Rather, they were to engage in this spiritual habit privately and the Father would reward them (Matthew 6:16-18). Also, Jesus told his disciples that certain things could happen only through fasting and prayer (Mark 9:29 NKJV). We can gain clarity and discern the timing or cadence of heaven more easily when we fast and pray. Jesus fasted and prayed for forty days before engaging in explosive, apostolic ministry (Matthew 4:1-12).

Similarly, Paul wanted the church to be in a place of continued encounter with God just as Jesus had revealed it through his own life. So Paul called the church to fast and pray often. Essentially, Paul was practicing a known Hebrew discipline but through the way of Jesus. We see that Paul fasted for three days after his dramatic, blinding encounter with Jesus on the Damascus Road (Acts 9:9). From that moment onward, Paul continued that rhythm to see and hear Jesus more clearly.

Also, it was in a season of fasting and prayer that the elders of Antioch heard from the Holy Spirit that Paul and Barnabas were being called into a powerful missionary journey (Acts 13:1-3). Even during his time on the hectic seas in a sinking ship, Paul fasted and prayed to hear the Lord clearly (Acts 27:21). Furthermore, in each of these cities with fledgling churches, Paul and Barnabas would pray and fast before appointing church leaders (Acts 14:23).

As you consider your own daily spiritual habits, what would it look like for you to establish habits of encounter on a regular basis? Chapters three and four are filled with potential habits that could be practiced daily, weekly, or in special seasons. Like Paul and these small church communities, you can lock into the cadence of heaven as you engage in the habit of encounter.

Habits of exploring: proclamation and testimony. Second, Paul established habits of exploring through proclaiming and testifying. Jesus made it clear that his disciples would be given opportunities to share their testimony and the message of the kingdom to all kinds of people. Jesus told them not to worry because the Holy Spirit would teach them what to say (Luke 12:11-12). Similarly, Jesus told the healed demoniac to go back into Decapolis and tell his friends what God had done for him (Mark 5:19).

Paul took this habit seriously. During any kind of gathering, he would report and testify about the grace and mercy of God through Jesus Christ (Acts 14:27; 15:4; 20:20, 27). What does it mean to report and testify? It means we talk openly and honestly about all the things we see God doing in and around us.

Why should we continue this practice?

Proclaiming and testifying helps us explore what God is doing in the lives of people. Our habits of testifying can pique spiritual curiosity in others, drawing out people of peace in whom God is already at work. Our testifying helps us remind one another that God is faithful. Our testifying magnifies the grace and mercy of God, in Jesus, working in our midst. Our testifying shows others that we are in this process together. Our testimony gives us time to celebrate.

As you consider your own daily spiritual habits, what would it look like for you to establish habits of exploring on a regular basis? Chapters five and six have great insight on how to explore what God is doing in a place and how to meet new people and explore what God is doing in their lives. Like Jesus and Paul showed us, we believe you can walk into *kairos* moments as you establish rhythms of exploring with those around you.

Habits of empowering: multiplying leaders. Last, Paul followed Jesus' example and established habits of empowering by multiplying leaders. Jesus appointed leaders and entrusted his mission to twelve apostles, seventy-two disciples, and one hundred and twenty followers. Jesus did not consider empowerment as a one-time experience, but it was a key habit in his ministry (Mark 3:13-19; Luke 6:12-19; 10:1-23; Acts 1:15).

Again, Paul did the same thing everywhere he went: he appointed leaders. He appointed and empowered Timothy, Onesimus, Silas, Aquila and Priscilla, Lydia, and many more. These leaders were empowered by the Spirit, and each was sent and supported by Paul to propagate the gospel into their communities.

As the mission grows around us, leaders and colaborers must be released and empowered to continue to match the momentum and cadence of the mission God is initiating. If we stop this habit, we stunt the potential of the community to make a lasting change. If we stop this rhythm, we create stagnant institutions and monuments for a few leaders. If we stop, we double down on the pervasive, consumerist ideology governing our cultural moment. We need to establish empowerment as an ongoing habit.

We establish rhythms of empowerment not simply for organizational or social reasons, but because of the deeply spiritual and theological belief in the priesthood of believers and the diverse, wondrous body of Christ we are becoming. Every time we empower a leader, we proclaim our belief in God's work in other people, not simply in our own lives. Again, this practice brings more people in sync with the cadence of heaven in a specific place and time.

As you consider your own daily spiritual habits, what would it look like for you to establish habits of empowerment? Chapters seven and eight provide key tools so you can pass on what you have to others. Like Jesus and Paul showed us, this reviving mission is for everyone, not just a few. Who could you invest in this week?

Make a list of your personal Timothy, Lydia, Silas, and Priscilla and Aquila. They are around you, so make it an ongoing habit to see them, develop them, and release them.

FORMING HABITS THAT STICK

It can be exciting to try living out new habits of encounter with God, exploring what God is doing, and empowering people. But how do we make these habits lead to lasting change? Let's return to James Clear's work to gain insight on how to help habits stick. Clear argues that for any practice to become a lasting habit in our lives, it needs to be obvious, attractive, easy, and satisfying.[6]

While this is not the only way to create and establish habits, it is a helpful place to start. So what can we do to make our habits of encounter (or explore or empower) more obvious, attractive, easy, and satisfying in our lives and in our communities? There is no one way! The answer to this question will depend on your personality and your community.

For example, let's take the specific encounter habit of seeking God daily and see how you could make that habit more obvious, attractive, easy, and satisfying.

How can you make the habit of seeking God daily more obvious in the rhythms of your day? Set an alarm on your phone to go on a walk daily and pray. Ask the Lord to meet you in a fresh way. It may be amazing or it may feel mundane. But you keep showing up to awaken yourself to his movement around you.

How can you make this habit attractive? You've been wanting to try a few trails near your house, so now is your chance to go. If you are an extrovert, invite a friend to join you so you'll look forward to your prayer walk.

How can you make it easy? Put your shoes, journal, and favorite pen in a bin next to the door. Then when the alarm goes off, you can move quickly to the door and have all your tools and gear in one place. If there are other obstacles to practicing the habit of seeking God daily, consider what you could do to minimize those obstacles. Make it easy!

How can you make the habit of seeking God daily satisfying? Create a chart or habit trackers inside your journal that you can mark to see your progress. If you don't like trackers, add a coffee shop at the end of your walk so you can get that drink you like.

In this example you are trying to establish one habit that will lead you to more encounter with God in your life. As this habit becomes consistent, your attentiveness will increase, you'll become more receptive, and you'll open yourself up to *kairos* moments of breakthrough with God.

Consider how you can use this framework for the other *E*s listed in this book. Recruit friends, family, or church members to join you in establishing habits like these. Encourage one another to keep at it. Do not weary in doing good. And don't feel locked into one habit for a particular one of the *E*s; feel free to change things up, but keep encountering, exploring, and empowering. It's in these small, established habits that God will awaken you and others around you to his reviving mission. (More resources on habits are available on our website, www.revivingmission.org.)

LONG-TERM IMPACT OF UNNOTICEABLE HABITS

None of these habits seems earth-shattering or novel. Yes, that is true. That's actually the point! That's how habits work. Habits can seem small and trivial, but when a community of people practice everyday habits in the places they inhabit, whole communities are transformed!

Consider the impact of the small fledgling communities of the early church scattered across Turkey, Italy, and the Mediterranean. These small communities spread through the entire Roman Empire and beyond, growing from twenty-five thousand to twenty million people in the span of just two hundred years.[7] How did they do this? According to historian Alan Kreider, it was everyday people embodying the ways of Jesus in their habits. Kreider refers to the slow, everyday, communal influence of habits as "patient ferment." Like yeast, their everyday existence in a particular place was used by God to transform the world around them.

In his book *The Patient Ferment of the Early Church*, Kreider describes this impact further: "Christians' focus was not on 'saving' people or recruiting them; it was on living faithfully—in the belief that when people's lives are rehabituated in the way of Jesus, others will want to join them."[8] It was their *habitus*, their way of life, that convinced people that Jesus was the way to eternal life. These everyday, equitable, patient rhythms and habits drew many into their communities as they modeled a different way of life—one that was attractive and subterranean at the same time. Much like Jesus' call to be the salt of the earth (Matthew 5:13) or his parable that the kingdom of God is like yeast (Matthew 13:33), these important influences are often unseen, but their impact is undeniable!

Sociologist Rodney Stark addresses this same dynamic, again pointing to the way of life of the early Christian communities as their strongest influence:

> Christianity revitalized life in Greco-Roman cities by providing new norms and new kinds of social relationships able to cope with many urgent urban problems. To cities filled with the homeless and impoverished, Christianity offered charity as well as hope. To cities filled with newcomers and strangers, Christianity offered an immediate basis for attachments. To cities filled with orphans and widows, Christianity provided a new and expanded sense of family. To cities torn

by violent ethnic strife, Christianity offered a new basis for social solidarity. And to cities faced with epidemics, fires, and earthquakes, Christianity offered effective nursing services.[9]

It seems that Jesus, Paul, and the early church were not passing along a system per se, but a way of life, a series of habits that could be employed within a community in a flexible, organic way. Jesus did not seem to care much about the static machinery or the individual cogs of a well-oiled machine, but rather he focused on giving people living seeds (habits) to plant in foreign soil to see the kingdom of God grow. In this way, Jesus and Paul were making the community resilient.

The same can be true for you and your community. Sure, these spiritual habits and rhythms may not be flashy or even noticed by those around us, but over time, they awaken us to God's everyday movement and we too become resilient. Entire communities and cities are changed when generations practice habits together in the places they inhabit.

ARE WE JUST GOING TO KEEP PRAYING?

Our (Linson's) church could see that the South Asian population of the Dallas–Ft. Worth Metroplex (DFW) was growing by leaps and bounds. We watched as Indians, Pakistanis, Nepalis, Sri Lankans, and Bangladeshis moved into our neighborhoods. High-tech companies were moving into Dallas and brand-new hospitals were being built everywhere; therefore, along with many others, South Asians were moving to DFW and being hired rapidly.

As we explored more of the city, we met a city councilman who shared another insight into why so many South Asians had moved into the area. He recounted a story of a famous Hindu swami from India who came to Texas and pronounced a blessing over a specific suburb in DFW. As news of his blessing spread throughout

South Asian communities in America and India, it drove even more migration.

We knew that God was moving and that he was calling us to invest in this growing community. So we prayed. Some of us became frustrated when it felt like all we were doing was praying and nothing was really happening.

"Are we just going to keep praying?" we wondered. "What should we actually do?"

But it was as we prayed that we heard God's voice affirming the call to plant a new church in this growing South Asian neighborhood. In this season of growing conviction of our calling, we encouraged one another by saying, "Yes, God's voice is clear even though the vision is not." We sensed that God was relocating the mission field while reenergizing the mission force in our city.

During yet another prayer meeting, we were inspired by the Spirit in a profound way as we read Acts 16:13-15. We read about the Macedonian call and the woman named Lydia who opened up new networks for the birth of the church in Philippi. We prayed earnestly for God to lead us to someone like Lydia who could open this new suburb for church planting by extending to us their networks and relational resources.

Then during a prayer drive (yes, more praying) around the city, our newly formed planting team was prompted by the Spirit to walk into a random coffee shop. Little did we know that God was at work and about to answer our prayers.

As soon as the planting team met the owner of the coffee shop, they called me to share the news that we had just found our Lydia! It turned out that our Lydia was a South Asian male named Suresh with a generous spirit and positive outlook on life. I was thrilled to meet Suresh and hear his story.

As we got to know Suresh, we learned that he was not a coffee connoisseur by any stretch of the imagination. He opened the coffee shop because he and his father, who is a missionary in India, felt led by God to open a coffee shop with the explicit purpose of creating space for any kind of ministry that might need it—especially a church plant wanting to reach South Asians. We saw a *kairos* moment unfolding before our eyes.

Suresh graciously opened his coffee shop to us to host Bible studies and, yes, more prayer meetings. He opened his network and introduced us to many people in the city. The planting team prayed, worshiped, and studied the Scriptures weekly with Suresh and others in that coffee shop. We established habits of encounter, exploring, and empowerment in this new place—a coffee shop in the heart of the neighborhood God had called us to.

As I reflect on this story, I feel struck that the one habit we constantly embodied was prayer. Our church prayed for years. At times it felt arduous. But it was during these everyday rhythms of prayer that God met us, led us, and clarified our calling. In one prayer time we heard only part of the vision. Then during a prayer meeting we received the next part of the plan. When we finally met Suresh (on a prayer drive), we started ongoing habits of prayer in his coffee shop. It was critical for us to establish these everyday habits of prayer because at every stage they opened us up to more and more *kairos* moments of breakthrough. These habits taught us to be resilient and gave us the opportunity to be in sync with the cadence of heaven.

4Es — ENCOUNTER — EXPLORE — EMPOWER — ESTABLISH

10

ESTABLISH

God of the Garden-City

SEVERAL YEARS AGO, my (Linson's) in-laws bought a new home with a huge backyard. As my son and I walked around the property, I gazed at their yard and wondered what they might do with it. My son exclaimed, "Grandma, what are you going to do with this big backyard?"

She laughed and said, "Oh, you will see!"

As it was, the backyard featured patches of grass, wildflowers scattered and strewn across the property, and random shrubs of mint. Everything was growing all on its own in an unorganized way. I am a terrible gardener, and had it been my backyard, I probably wouldn't have given it another thought. The plants there might have continued to live, but they certainly would haven't thrived.

However, my mother-in-law has a green thumb. Actually, that is an understatement—she can make anything grow. Literally. She took my dying *kariveppila* plant, also known as a curry leaf plant, and brought it back to life with a few eggshells and banana peels. She has an incredible gift. Occasionally she brings me an assortment of flowers that she propagated so I can plant them at my house. Unfortunately, after a few weeks or so under my care, those flowers have withered and died (as I said, I am a terrible gardener).

Several months after they moved into their house, I went back to visit. I walked into their backyard, and I was amazed. It had been transformed into an incredible garden with vegetables, fruits, and flowers of all kinds. There were wooden trellises, raised garden beds, garden arches, and plants in various-sized pots in a makeshift greenhouse.

As I was exploring the garden, I heard my mother-in-law's voice from somewhere behind a blossoming plant. She was calling me to help her harvest okra, green beans, tomatoes, bell peppers, serrano peppers, eggplants, figs, and much more. I brought all of the produce into the house. My son exclaimed, "You got all this from your backyard?"

My mother-in-law said, "I told you. I had a plan!"

Gardeners matter! Sure, the backyard was alive in its wild, untouched state. But it became something beautiful after it came under my mother-in-law's care. It became fruitful and productive, and it yielded more than it could have on its own.

For that to happen, the backyard required my mother-in-law's intervention and cultivation. As she worked on it, it began to feel both organic and structured simultaneously. It conveyed the desire, design, intention, and plans of a gardener. It became a habitat for life.

My mother-in-law gives me a glimpse into the personality of God. He too creates systems for organic growth. He builds dynamic structures for life to flourish. He makes things beautiful. His habitats are fluid, natural, structured, strong, and resilient. He is a master gardener-architect. He is the God of the garden-city.

GOD OF THE GARDEN-CITY

God creates habitats. Consider the creation narrative as God takes what is formless and empty and infuses it with fullness (Genesis 1:2). Three times in the creation story God creates habitats and then fills them with life. First, he creates light and darkness and fills them with the sun, moon, and stars (Genesis 1:3, 14-19). Second, he creates the sky and the waters and fills them with birds and fish (Genesis 1:6-8, 20-23). Third, he creates the dry land and fills it with vegetation, wild animals, insects, and livestock of all kinds (Genesis 1:9-13, 24-25). God creates habitats that foster life and fullness.

In Genesis 2, God creates the Garden of Eden for humanity to be safe, situated, and sent to fill the entire earth with life, ideas, and culture (Genesis 1:26-31). Notice the garden is organized and cultivated. God's habitat is not chaotic (Genesis 2:8-15). This idea is perfectly articulated by Bruce Waltke, Old Testament professor and author, when he states, "[The garden] denotes an enclosed, protected area where the flora flourishes. It represents territorial space in the created order where God invites human beings to enjoy bliss and harmony between themselves and God, one another, animals, and the land. God is uniquely present here. The Garden of Eden is a temple-garden."[1] We see the nature of God in his creation of this holy and sublime habitat.

The prophet Isaiah reveals God's heart to create a habitat for the people of Israel by using the metaphor of a vineyard. In the story a man finds the perfect place for the vineyard to be planted, he digs and clears it of stones, he plants the choicest of vines, and he sets up a wall, a watchtower, and a winepress (Isaiah 5:1-4). This parable describes the loving, tender care of God as our gardener and architect.

In the New Testament, we see the theme of habitats continue as God plans to build his people into a temple of living stones with Jesus Christ as the cornerstone (1 Peter 2:4-5). At the culmination of history, there is a grand city of God constructed with precious jewels and gold. There is no temple, but it is a habitat for his people to dwell forever (Revelation 21:10-27). This evokes images of God as a skillful architect, or even a lavish custom home designer and general contractor. Beautiful does not even come close to describing the habitat in store for us as his children.

Jürgen Moltmann, theologian and author, takes the concept further by stating that, surprisingly, God is also creating a habitat for himself. Moltmann writes, "In the end, however, the new heaven and the new earth will become the temple of God's indwelling. The whole world will become God's home.... The whole creation will be transfigured through the indwelling of God's glory."[2] That is an incredible idea. God creates a habitat even for his own presence. His presence makes all things new.

There is one more masterful move that God makes. He restores Eden amid the architecture of the Holy City. God brings back the garden within the city! Consider how beautiful it is that God replants the tree of life—a tree that bears twelve crops of fruit and whose leaves are used for healing the nations (Revelation 22:2). Consider that God, in Christ Jesus, has removed the curse that kept us away from his presence (Revelation 22:3). Humanity is allowed to commune with God again, face-to-face.[3] We can walk the streets of gold and walk in the garden in the cool of the day. Past, present, and future collide as Genesis meets Revelation and what's old is made new again. We rejoice at the marvelous story arc that brings God's people back to the garden to be with him.

God creates spaces for himself and his people that connect magnificent architecture with the fluidity and life of a well-watered garden. The tensions of boundaries and growth, order and multiplication, resilience and flexibility are brought into harmony and evoke beauty beyond imagination. From the beginning to the end of the scriptural narrative it's clear—God creates beautiful habitats.

JESUS ESTABLISHED GROUPS TO INITIATE THE MOVEMENT

Jesus also expresses the image of God the gardener-architect when he creates not just physical but social habitats. Through the genius of Jesus, communities become habitats where his reviving mission can take root and flourish.

First, Jesus chooses the twelve. This group was selected to spend time with Jesus, to accompany him on his mission, to be sent out to new places, and to be given authority (Mark 3:13-19). Jesus creates this *personal* space to be a place of relationship, modeling, and learning. The twelve encounter God, explore new communities, and empower others as the movement grows across Judea. Along the way they grow in friendship with one another and with Jesus.

Next, Jesus chooses three from within the twelve—namely, Peter, James, and John—to form an *intimate* space. This group experiences moments the twelve did not. They are with Jesus as he is transfigured (Mark 9:2-8), they are in the room when Jairus's daughter is resurrected (Mark 5:21-43), and they are called to go deeper in the garden of Gethsemane to pray with Jesus (Mark 14:32-34). Jesus creates this intimate space for deeper revelation and increased access.

Next, we see Jesus send out the seventy-two in pairs to different towns and villages in Judea (Luke 10:1-23), and it is probable that these seventy-two are included in the one hundred and twenty praying in the upper room at Pentecost (Acts 1:15). This larger *social* space is one of broad mobilization into mission, collective spiritual momentum, and experiences of rejoicing.

Last, Jesus interacts with the crowds, which are typically made up of a wide diversity of people, including seekers and skeptics, the hyper-religious and the ritually impure, the elite and the outcast. They gather to hear Jesus preach, observe him do miracles, and even watch him break cultural protocols. Jesus has compassion on the crowds. He sees them as lost without any guidance. Jesus uses this *public* space to practice compassion, preach about the kingdom, and provoke curiosity.

Jesus establishes these different social habitats so the movement will grow and then continue after his departure. These spaces are essential for him to transfer his reviving mission on to others. Each of these social habitats facilitates unique habits and spiritual rhythms. Often, different but overlapping habits are practiced within each space. Why does Jesus do this? Because he is not only fostering life; he is also organizing it.

PAUL ESTABLISHED GROUPS TO BUILD THE MOVEMENT

Paul followed the pattern laid out by Jesus and continued to build the movement by using similar social spaces as habitats.

Like Jesus, Paul was a part of a *personal* space that included a handful of companions. We see one such habitat in the leadership team at Antioch (Acts 13:1-3), we see another in the missionary teams that traveled with him through Asia Minor (Acts 16:6) and Macedonia (Acts 20:4-6), and we also see that Paul lists several groups within his letters. Though it was less defined—particularly as Paul's journeys took him across the Mediterranean world—this habitat mimics the personal space of the twelve that Jesus created.

Paul was also part of a smaller *intimate* group as he worked closely and even one-on-one with partners like Barnabas, Timothy, Silas, and Priscilla and Aquila. They experienced moments together that his other companions did not, whether moments of great joy as they saw new faith communities started or moments of conflict, suffering, persecution, and imprisonment. This was an intimate space of a few people who built long-lasting friendship and partnership despite the hardships they endured.

Next, Paul and the other leaders of the church utilized a *social* habitat called *oikos*, which is a Greek word meaning "household." *Oikos* describes all the people in or around a dwelling that formed a family unit comprising men, women, children, servants, neighbors, friends, and so on.[4] *Oikos* shows up repeatedly in the New Testament in the stories of Cornelius (Acts 10), Lydia (Acts 16), Crispus (Acts 18:8), Onesiphorus (2 Timothy 4:19), and more.

Last, Paul consistently engaged *public* spaces like the marketplace (Acts 17:17), synagogues (Acts 19:8), the Hall of Tyrannus in Ephesus (Acts 19:9), the Areopagus in Athens (Acts 17:22), and other similar spaces to preach, debate, and provoke curiosity. Paul engaged this space in a similar way to how Jesus interacted with the crowds.

As both Jesus and Paul expressed God's reviving mission, we can see the ways they formed social spaces into habitats to hold the everyday movement of God. Rather than a one-size-fits-all approach, they invested in different types of social spaces and capitalized on the ways those spaces might be leveraged to grow the resilience of the communities they were starting. Temple was not better than homes, nor was the synagogue better than the marketplace. Large crowds were not better than one-on-one conversations. Each type of space was significant. The reviving mission of Jesus expressed across all of these social habitats fostered resilience.

FOUR SOCIAL HABITATS

Jesus was a genius of creating different spaces and social habitats. Jesus had the three, the twelve, the seventy (rounded), and the crowds. Paul followed Jesus' example and had an inner circle of colaborers, a traveling band of missionaries, *oikos* communities, and the synagogue or marketplace. The genius of Jesus and Paul is further confirmed by the teachings of modern sociology, which

Establish: God of the Garden-City 183

point to these same kinds of social spaces as foundational to our relational lives.

In their book *Church as Movement*, JR Woodward and Dan White Jr. describe the four spaces of belonging, adapted from the work of sociologist Edward T. Hall and author Joseph Myers: "Each space—intimate, personal, social, and public—is designed to deliver something the other spaces can't deliver by themselves."[5]

SPACES OF BELONGING

	Intimate space	Personal space	Social space	Public space
Group size	2-5	5-20	20-70	70+
Jesus	Peter, James, John — Experienced unique and important moments with Jesus	The twelve disciples — Called to be with Jesus and to be sent out with authority	The seventy household (*Oikos*) Attractive communities that reached networks	The crowds — Jesus taught in parables, preached about, and demonstrated the kingdom of God
Paul	Paul and Barnabas — Priscilla and Aquila	Elders in Antioch — Traveling missionary band	House churches (*Oikos*)	Synagogue — Marketplace
Strength	Vulnerability and accountability	Discipleship and modeling	Mission and attraction	Vision and communal encounter with God
Limitation	High cost of joining	Can be insular	Difficult to be vulnerable	Not the ideal place for discipleship
Potential structures	Mentoring relationship — Accountability partner — Marriages — Close friendships	Smaller small group — Smaller ministry team — Cohort	Larger small group — Missional community — Larger ministry team — Class	Worship service — Outreach event — Conference

Figure 10.1. The four spaces of belonging

Intimate spaces are the most vulnerable (and the most private) spaces and include only a few folks—spouses, parents, children, important mentoring relationships, and the closest of friends (see fig. 10.1[6]). *Personal* spaces are typically close groups of five to twenty people. These spaces include close coworkers, friends, and small groups or ministry teams. *Social* spaces are places of broad relational connection like parties, larger leadership gatherings, classrooms, and midsized missional communities. *Public* spaces are open and filled with a crowd, much like worship services or large outreach events.

As we examined above, Jesus and Paul used public spaces as they engaged the crowds gathered in the countryside, synagogues, or marketplaces. They regularly engaged social spaces as they ministered in households and empowered groups of people like the seventy-two. Each used personal spaces, whether the twelve disciples or Paul's missionary teams, and each also had intimate spaces of deep partnership with trusted friends like James, John, and Peter, or Barnabas and Timothy.

THE HABITATS OF OUR LIVES

So what does that mean for our everyday lives?

On one level, we already inhabit these kinds of spaces every day, but we have a choice as to how we engage them. We can either go in and out of these social habitats mindlessly, or we can utilize them like Jesus and Paul did. We have the opportunity to get involved in these habitats. Like master gardener-architects, we can cultivate life by filling these habitats with life-giving habits like prayer, curiosity, encouragement, and service. Said differently, we can influence and shape social spaces so they will be more attuned or awakened to the movement of God.

How might things change if you considered your work environment as a social habitat that Jesus wanted you to "garden" and fill with life and flourishing? How might your coworkers encounter

God and experience glimpses of the kingdom if you prayed for and blessed your colleagues?

How might you think about your family as a social habitat that Jesus is cultivating through the everyday habits you practice there? Whether praying with your kids at night, spending time meeting neighbors on your street, joining the soccer team to meet new people, or going on dates with your spouse, this too is a place to grow expressions of God's kingdom that bear the fruit of the Spirit.

Our lives flourish as we inhabit each of these kinds of spaces, and beyond how we might influence these spaces with the reviving mission of Jesus, we need expressions of each of these spaces in our lives in order to build resilience.

Sure, you might be an extrovert and uncomfortable in intimate spaces, but we believe Jesus has something special for you there as you build deep, transparent friendships. Vice versa, you might be an introvert and cringe as you consider your next social gathering, but how might God use you to fill that habitat with his presence?

RESILIENCE IN VOLATILE ENVIRONMENTS

Beyond the ways we all naturally inhabit these spaces in our everyday lives, embracing the reviving mission of Jesus means intentionally creating these kinds of social habitats to foster the life of the kingdom, even in the midst of *volatility*.

The Greco-Roman world was a volatile place filled with revolutionary leaders, insurgents, and empire builders. Yet amid that chaos, the kingdom of God was inhabiting different kinds of social spaces. Both Jesus and Paul would use these spaces to facilitate encounters, explore networks, and empower leaders. These varied spaces did not slow the movement of God; rather, they provided the resilience needed for the people of God to thrive in any kind of situation.

It is remarkable to see how Jesus and Paul established rhythms of ongoing encounter, exploration, and empowerment in so many different ways. They gave people endless possibilities to embody these rhythms regardless of how volatile the circumstances became. The nascent church could innovate and bring habits into new habitats to adjust to their surroundings. The habits endured no matter the environment. Powerful resilience was being cultivated within the movement that transcended the fragility produced by the volatile systems of the day.

Volatility is always around us. We cannot ignore it. We see it on the news; we experience it at work, at church, and on different social media platforms. This volatility causes anxiety, fear, and fragility within us and others if we are not mindful of it.

The US Navy SEALs have a concept called "VUCA" that helps explain the circumstances surrounding organizations, churches, and communities in this cultural moment. This acronym stands for volatile, uncertain, complex, and ambiguous. Navy SEALs train for difficult environments and assume they are entering a VUCA reality no matter what it might seem like initially.[7]

I cannot think of a better way of explaining ministry in the post-pandemic, post-Christian world in which we live. Our world is marked by experiences of fragility and everything seems to be turning upside down in industry, religion, politics, culture, and our interpersonal interactions. It is no wonder many of us have turned to deconstruction or thrown up our hands in resignation.

THE HABITATS WE CREATE

So what do we do in light of the volatility of our context? How do we foster the flourishing of our communities despite the challenges of this cultural moment?

We need to embrace the resilience that Jesus and Paul provide us by creating habitats that can steward the reviving mission of God in different social spaces. We need to embrace the way of the master gardener-architect. What does that look like for you and me?

Several researchers, social scientists, and thinkers help shape our ideas about resilience and organizational structures. Some of their ideas can be used to help us establish resilient habitats for our communities.

Steven Johnson, author and theorist, suggests that resilient life is formed in "liquid" spaces that have equal measures of structure and fluidity. In contrast to "solid" spaces that are too rigid to adapt to change and "gaseous" spaces that are too chaotic to sustain enduring life, Johnson argues that "liquid" habitats can adapt to their context while maintaining cohesion.[8]

How might this apply to the church? We believe that this theory describes the genius of Jesus, the way of the master gardener-architect, because it embraces both organic flow and structural integrity. Essentially, we need to be able to create habitats that are structured enough to provide support and stability but flexible enough to adapt to change. We need "liquid" habitats to thwart the impact of volatility and the pull toward fragility.

Similarly, Nassim Nicholas Taleb, essayist and mathematical statistician, introduces the concept of antifragility. He explains that there are things in nature that are not fragile nor rigid but have an important third quality: *antifragility*. He states, "Antifragility is beyond resilience or robustness. The resilient resists shocks and stays the same; the antifragile gets better. . . . Some things benefit from shocks; they thrive and grow when exposed to volatility, randomness, disorder, and stressors and love adventure, risk, and uncertainty."[9] Taleb argues that we need more than mere resilience, because some things don't just survive volatility; they thrive on it.

Can this be applied to the church? As we examine Jesus and Paul's ministry, we see the constant persecution, uncertainty, threats, and obstacles they faced. During that time the movement did not become rigid, nor did it become weak or fragile—it became better. In America, we do not face the same kinds of hardship that confronted the early church or many of our sisters and brothers around the world, but we do face the fragility that comes with the post-pandemic world. Just like the early church became stronger and antifragile, we can help our faith communities do the same through leveraging the power of social habitats.

As we design habitats to foster resilience, it's essential that we recognize that different habits can express themselves in different social spaces—there is no one-size-fits-all approach to embedding habits in habitats. For example, suggesting that prayer can happen only in intimate, private space limits what God can do and diminishes the resilience of our communities. Assuming that public outreach events are the only place for witness compromises multifaceted avenues for exploration.

Similarly, we cannot merely stick to one kind of habit and use it exclusively across every habitat. We have friends who think prayer is the only thing we need to do at church. They think we should pray alone, pray in small groups, pray at social events, and pray during our Sunday morning services—whatever the question is, prayer is the answer. While we hope you've heard from us how critical we think prayer is, habitats don't thrive without biodiversity. To be sure, communities need to pray, but they also need to connect with each other, bear witness, be trained, and so on.

Finally, we cannot expect a single habitat to carry all the habits a community needs to flourish in resilience. Some churches ask their Sunday morning services (typically a public or social space) to do everything—help people encounter God, serve as a venue for outreach, become a platform for leadership—all while fostering deep, transformational community. Just as healthy environments need "habit" diversity (e.g., we need to do more than pray), so too do they need "habitat" diversity—we can't assume one structure is sufficient for every need.

The habitats we create must evolve and embody the way of the master gardener-architect. We must make room for adaptation and liquidity. Our communities must be liquid—not too rigid but not too chaotic, structured enough to sustain but flexible enough to adapt. In a volatile world that creates fear and propagates fragility, we can partner with the God of the garden-city to create living systems and organic structures.

ESTABLISH RESILIENT STRUCTURES IN YOUR COMMUNITY

Since churches, ministries, and small groups grow and develop at different rates and are made up of different kinds of people, it is important to experiment with how to embed habits in different habitats, and this takes discernment.

It can feel tricky at first, but let's try it together.

Perhaps you want to see your community grow in the habits of empowerment—you want to see leaders developed and equipped for ministry. You could locate these habits of empowerment in an intimate, personal, social, or public space. Which would work best for your community?

Let's imagine empower in all four spaces and consider what might work best.

Empower + intimate space. You could locate empower habits in the intimate space. You could invest in people through one-on-one discipleship relationships and help your friend grow their authority through the power equation.

Empower + personal space. You could locate empower habits in the personal space. You could train your small group on having spiritual conversations and then practice together to grow your skill.

Empower + social space. Empower habits could be practiced in the social space, perhaps the leadership team at your church. You could spend time identifying other potential leaders in your community and then praying together for those emerging leaders.

Empower + public space. Empower habits could be practiced in the public space. You could challenge your whole community by hosting a large-scale event at the church focused on the theme of consecration. People could worship, hear an inspiring message, and then receive prayer for empowerment.

Each of these strategies is a viable way to invest in the empowerment of your community—it's up to you to prayerfully decide which strategy would be best, and, of course, it's possible you will need several strategies working together to see the resilience God desires in you and your community.

This is just one example that illustrates the ways we can leverage habitats to grow our communities in the reviving mission of Jesus. (Please go to www.revivingmission.org for more examples of this kind of thinking and concrete ideas of other habit and habitat combinations.)

RECOGNIZING THE STRENGTHS AND LIMITATIONS OF DIFFERENT SPACES

While we do believe that you can embed different habits in each of the four types of spaces, it's also important to recognize the unique strengths and limitations of each space. Some things happen better in a group of four than in a group of forty. Woodward and White make this clear:

> One size does not fit all. There is nothing more frustrating than trying to produce certain kinds of relational experiences from a group not designed to deliver them. When helping people navigate their journey into experiencing community, it's important for them to recognize the nature—the benefits and their inherent limitations—of these four spaces. This means helping people set appropriate relational expectations for each space.[10]

Intimate spaces, for example, are an ideal habitat for vulnerability. Utilizing accountability partnerships or mentoring pairs is a great way to create intimate spaces that foster honesty and vulnerability about what's really going on in people's lives. Intimate spaces are naturally limited in that they require a high degree of trust. This means they can be difficult to access for new people, so don't make an intimate habitat the first or primary way for new people to explore your community.

Personal spaces present the ideal habitat for discipleship. There's a reason Jesus chose to invest in twelve disciples. A community this size can expect a lot from one another, hold each other accountable, and create opportunities for modeling and learning a way of life. A word of invitation here: Many churches and ministries limit discipleship to one-on-one conversations at a coffee shop. Let's expand our ideas about discipleship and embrace Jesus' example of gathering a community to learn a way of life and practice it together. A limitation of personal space is that on its own, it can become insular. That's why we need social spaces to help us continue to expand our relationships.

Social spaces present the strongest habitat for a community to engage in mission, whether in a neighborhood, a network, or a campus. Woodward and White write, "Social space is small enough for people to experience authentic community, but big enough to mobilize people for missional movement."[11] A social space brings relational momentum and critical mass while still giving access to genuine experiences of community. A limitation of the social space as a habitat is that it's too large for vulnerability and accountability. Another word of invitation: This is an underutilized space in most churches and ministries. Many communities leave a gap between small group Bible studies with ten people and larger worship gatherings of a hundred or more. A community of forty people is a missional force! Don't overlook these midsized communities; they are the most potent habitat for engaging a place with the reviving mission of Jesus.

Public spaces are an ideal habitat for shaping the imagination of a community. Gatherings such as worship services and large group fellowship meetings are a great place to share stories of how mission is progressing in a place (probably through personal and social spaces). This inspires people and builds momentum for the broader community. Public spaces are also great for sharing big vision and creating space for a whole community to encounter God in worship. However, public space is very limited in its ability to foster community or any kind of relational interaction. People can hear information in a public space, but they can't watch someone live out a way of life. It's hard to ask someone to be vulnerable in a room of potentially hundreds of people. This is why Jesus didn't disciple the crowds. He provoked curiosity and cast vision about the kingdom of God in these spaces. But we need to recognize the limitations of public space.

SIGNS OF RESILIENCE WHEN ESTABLISHING STRUCTURES

Since there are so many combinations of habits within habitats, how do we know if we are doing it right? Though there are several indicators of health, here are four kinds of fruit born from well-designed habitats.

First, we will notice that authority comes from integrity, not institutions. When a habitat grows stale, it can lead to unhelpful institutional centers of power. This kind of authority can create a rigid conformity to rules, political maneuvering, ambiguity leading to suspicion, or misplaced hope for its constituents. But in Jesus' reviving mission, it matters less if a person has institutional or organizational power, because having a genuine encounter with God expressed in a life of obedience becomes the source of true authority.

We are not at all saying institutions are inherently evil—organizations, churches, businesses, and more can be used by God to bring about the flourishing of others. But when our dependence on God, our obedience to God, and our affections for God are misshapen by institutional ideologies or are distracted by shallow sources of power, our authority becomes fragile and brittle. God, the master gardener-architect, desires for us to cultivate an authority found in knowing and encountering him. This is true resilience.

Second, our view of resources moves from scarcity to abundance. Sometimes we can overburden people by creating habitats that feel like we are running out of money, personnel, space, and so on. Scarcity is a mindset that can wreak havoc on even the most well-intentioned habitats. It can cause a community to wait for "enough" resources before they engage in Jesus' reviving mission. Scarcity is so powerful that it will convince us the right resources will never come. We will always feel like more money is needed, more logistics need to be planned, more people need to be recruited. We need more and more. When this happens, our engagement with others feels fragile, weak, and incomplete.

But in Jesus' reviving mission, our habitats help us embrace abundance and a mindset of generosity. Often this happens as we relocate habits into a better habitat. In so doing we can unlock resources, motivate people, and create momentum. This mentality is perfectly described by Neil Cole, pastor and author, who states, "All the resources we need will be found in the harvest."[12] Generosity is part of cultivating our resilience.

Third, our leadership models go from including a few to incorporating many. Jim Collins, researcher and author, reiterates that charismatic leaders can become "geniuses with a thousand volunteers" instead of becoming leaders who shape a culture that thrives beyond any one leader.[13] Often our spiritual communities drift toward the same style of solo or limited leadership. We will support one influential leader even when we see warning flags. But with the downfall of that one leader, entire communities are hurt and disillusioned, and many may turn away from Jesus. This kind of habitat is fragile and not marked by the resilience of our master gardener-architect.

In the reviving mission of Jesus, when our habitats are filled with people who are empowered by the Spirit, we begin to embrace the reality that the true fruit of leadership isn't more followers; it's more leaders! Our leadership habitats shift and morph to create space for many kinds of people who can lead mission together. Instead of feeling unhelpfully centralized, our leadership becomes polycentric and communal. Again, this model embraces the adaptability and resilience found in the leadership of Jesus.

Last, our partners evolve from competitors to collaborators. If we are not careful, our habitats can become echo chambers that reinforce our own opinions, biases, and sense of self. Before we know it, our practices, methods, and ideas are deemed normative, correct, and superior. These kinds of habitats will cause us to see others in the broader church as competitors instead of colaborers. These competitive habitats create boundaries that are overly distinct and no longer permeable. Ideas, people, and resources are constrained and unable to move between organizations to benefit the whole body. We become solid and not liquid networks. We choke ourselves and others when we do this. Our community becomes weak and fragile.

In the reviving mission of Jesus, our habitats extend and connect with others in collaborative ways. Though our distinctions do not disappear, we come into dialogue with others to create a culture that is less about protection and more about connection and shared innovation. Together we can see the whole mission of God in all its diversity and scope. We can see and celebrate the move of God in new geographies, ethnicities, and social circles. We will see habitats that incorporate our distinct borders but create the kind permeability that allows for entire ecosystems to be unleashed for the kingdom of God. This is the fingerprint of the master

Establish: God of the Garden-City

gardener-architect. This is truly a resilient expression of Christ in our world.

Will you be shrewd but also hold loosely the habitats of your community? Will you take on the calling of a master gardener-architect? Do not be afraid or paralyzed by the many possibilities, but instead be bold, humble, and willing to listen to the Lord and your community. Then, when you are ready, experiment with various habitats and habits. God wants to revive you and many around you. Work with the God of the garden-city to see his life and architecture be realized all around you.

ARE YOU CRAZY? HIRE MORE PEOPLE?

In 2019, my (Linson's) church was doing relatively well and growing slowly. But our stellar senior pastor was overworked and feeling the strain of a growing congregation. He and the other leaders of the church knew things could be better.

So in mid-2019, the church hired a student pastor, and in early 2020, I was hired as an associate pastor. We were able to diversify the leadership team and provide some much-needed bandwidth at the pastoral level. It was a huge move for our church as we'd had only one pastor for over three decades.

The week after I was hired, the world experienced the Covid-19 pandemic. I had one typical Sunday as a pastor, and then we had to shut down the church. As the months continued, we heard stories about churches going under, pastors quitting, and believers losing hope. The situation felt scarce and dire. Many wondered, "Are we crazy? Why did we hire more people?"

However, instead of staying in that place of fear, we decided we would trust the Lord in this terrible situation. I felt the Lord say that, like a caterpillar, we would build a chrysalis and emerge from it different. My senior pastor supported that sentiment when he said, "We hear his voice despite not having a clear vision." Together we shared this hope with our church leaders. We knew God would resurrect us into new life somehow.

Over the coming months we were forced to examine our organization and its habitats. We reorganized our ministry into new teams and appointed new leaders. We invested in new technology to serve our congregants as they were in lockdown. We had to learn new skills and invest into new kinds of leaders. This allowed us to release authority based on integrity and not institution.

Then, surprisingly, as told in chapter nine, we felt led by the Lord to plant another church despite the churches closing around us. We prayed regularly for this vision. We shifted resources to make this a reality. We trusted that God would bring resources from the harvest for the harvest. This allowed us to maintain an abundance mentality when surrounded by scarcity.

We collaborated with real estate agents, coffee shop owners, and local pastors and ministers to set up the new church. They helped us map out a planting strategy and find a great location. Together we encountered God, explored the city, and empowered more leaders. This allowed us to see others as collaborators, not competitors. We saw God soften hearts and build new partnerships.

Simultaneously, we noticed that the mother church was growing as we reopened the doors for in-person services. We heard many dechurched families say that they had watched us online for months during lockdown and decided we would be their new church home. We heard stories of young adults feeling far from God and deciding to come back to Christ again. We had to hire more staff to keep up with church growth.

It was then that I heard the familiar refrain from others in our congregation: "Pastor, are you sure? Hire more people?"

They were right in some ways. It would be financially stressful to hire more people. But also, culturally speaking, South Asian churches rarely hired more than one pastor and never hired nonpastoral staff. What we were proposing would fly in the face of convention. It would take bold humility to do this.

But after our community engaged in prayerful dialogue, God allowed us to hire several more staff members to serve both campuses. We were different ages, had different skill sets, and held different viewpoints, but God brought us together as a diverse leadership team. The church was strengthened as we invited staff to join us in the reviving mission of Jesus. This allowed us to create habitats that incorporated many leaders instead of just a few.

Now, by the grace of God, the church has doubled in size. God has granted us a new vision to plant two more churches, find new buildings for our current churches, and hire more staff and pastors. This is not happening because of our talent, skills, or genius. Quite the contrary! We decided to trust the God of the garden-city, to walk in the ways of the master gardener, to embrace the genius of Jesus, and to mimic the structures of Paul. We evaluated our systems and evolved our habitats in a way that helped us awaken to the everyday movement of God all around us.

Leading in the midst of volatility is tough, but God is raising up a resilient church all over the world. Jesus initiated a movement, Paul and others helped build that movement, and we have been given the great joy and responsibility to steward this movement into its future. One day we will all gather at the great garden-city designed by God, but until then, will you build habitats so that the people of God will flourish together?

ESTABLISH SUMMARY

Reviving mission establishes rhythms of community to help life flourish.

Who God is. As he demonstrated at creation when he established habitats and filled them with life, God is the master gardener-architect who is building a temple of living stones and designing a garden-city where he will dwell with his people and make all things new.

How we live. As people who bear his image, we are called to be like God in establishing rhythms of community so the life God gives can be fruitful and resilient. Though we live in a volatile world fraught with fragility, embracing the *kairos* and *chronos* cadence of God enables our communities to express the enduring resilience of Jesus.

What we do. As we practice habits and cultivate habitats to support the life of our communities, we begin to see the generational impact of consistent rhythms and signs of renewal that match the new season God is releasing in our day.

God's reviving mission is marked by resilience because it is embedded in the habits and habitats of established communal rhythms.

	WHO GOD IS	HOW WE LIVE	WHAT WE DO
ENCOUNTER God	God is here and God is moving.	Wonder versus cynicism	Seek God and respond to his movement.
EXPLORE what God is doing	God is the one who was, is, and is to come.	Curiosity versus contempt	Recognize God's three-dimensional work in places and people.
EMPOWER people	God gives his Spirit without measure.	Generosity versus narcissism	Serve and send people in the power of the Holy Spirit.
ESTABLISH rhythms of community	God is the master gardener-architect.	Resilience versus fragility	Practice habits and cultivate habitats.

Figure 10.2. Reviving mission grid—establish

Conclusion

THE JOY OF JESUS

It remains our conviction that God is doing something new in our day to both revitalize his people and revive his mission in the world. After a season of disruption that has eroded many of our cultural institutions and exposed counterfeit faith in the church, many of us are simultaneously weary of the status quo and hungry for a new way forward.

Thankfully, signs of a new season are emerging all around us. We believe God is inviting us as his followers to awaken to his everyday movement and embody the reviving mission of Jesus as sent ones in our workplaces, neighborhoods, and relational networks.

As we conclude this book, we want to summarize where we've been and offer a benediction as we look forward to the journey ahead.

RETRACING OUR STEPS

At the heart of this book is a framework called the 4*E*s that articulates a pattern of Jesus' reviving mission that we see replicated throughout the early church—encounter God, explore what he is doing, empower people, and establish communal rhythms.

What's more, we've proposed that these 4*E*s are a paradigm of holistic discipleship in that they each are rooted in the person of God (who God is), inform redemptive postures (how we live), and shape our everyday practices (what we do).

Just like new wine needs a new wineskin (Mark 2:22), we believe that the 4*E*s understood across these three levels articulate a model of reviving mission that matches the everyday movement of God in this moment and might be used by him to steward the seasonal shift that he is releasing in our day.

At their heart, the 4*E*s are a mystery that reveals something fundamentally beautiful about *who God is*. *Encounter* highlights for us the ways God is always near to us, but never in a stagnant way, because he is always on the move. He is here and he is moving, so there is no place where we cannot know him and encounter his presence. As we move with the God who moves we can experience his person in ever-deepening ways. *Explore* reminds us that God exists and acts in multidimensional ways that are not bound by time. He is the one who was and is and is to come—and he is the one who is actively at work in the present to both redeem the past and manifest his glorious future in the life of every person we meet and every place we inhabit. *Empower* helps us recognize that God doesn't just send us but in fact entrusts his very self to us through the person of the Holy Spirit. We are empowered without measure by the Spirit who saturates the whole of our lives and infuses us with supernatural authority to express his kingdom wherever we go. *Establish* helps us see God as the master gardener-architect who cultivates organic systems and grows living structures in which (or is it in whom?) he might live—a vital temple of living stones where his presence dwells.

At another level, the 4*E*s are a model that shapes redemptive postures for *how we live* as God's people in this cultural moment. Instead of the pervasive cynicism of our day, encountering God invites us to live lives saturated with wonder. In contrast to the judgmental contempt of our society, exploration invites us into a curiosity that helps us recognize God's movement anew, especially in places or among people who might surprise us. In place of a toxic narcissism that reinforces our own status, empowering others freely with what we have received begets generosity in our midst. Rather than the fragility that marks so many of our lives and institutions, establishing communal rhythms helps us cultivate a fundamental resiliency that can sustain the life that God gives.

Finally, the 4*E*s serve as a practical method for *what we do* to join Jesus' reviving mission wherever God might send us. Our first invitation is to encounter the God who is here through seeking him and responding to his movement all around us. Next, we explore by recognizing God's three-dimensional work—what he has done, is doing, and will do—in the places and among the people he has sent us to. Third, we empower others by serving and sending them in the power of the Holy Spirit generously given without measure. Finally, we establish rhythms of community by practicing habits and cultivating the habitats we need to experience the kind of enduring fruitfulness God desires. (For more practical resources and 4*E* tools, please visit our website www.revivingmission.org.)

	WHO GOD IS	HOW WE LIVE	WHAT WE DO
ENCOUNTER God	God is here and God is moving.	Wonder versus cynicism	Seek God and respond to his movement.
EXPLORE what God is doing	God is the one who was, is, and is to come.	Curiosity versus contempt	Recognize God's three-dimensional work in places and people.
EMPOWER people	God gives his Spirit without measure.	Generosity versus narcissism	Serve and send people in the power of the Holy Spirit.
ESTABLISH rhythms of community	God is the master gardener-architect.	Resilience versus fragility	Practice habits and cultivate habitats.

Figure C.1. Reviving mission grid—complete

Taken together, these ideas create a framework for reviving mission in our day. They help us revive our conception of mission in that they locate our work as a response to God's work, and they ensure that whatever we do in a place respects and amplifies what God is already doing there. What's more, they equip us as we join God's mission to revive the people and places he has called us to and become agents of revival who express his resurrection life wherever we go. Finally, they invite us to experience the ways Jesus' mission revives our own lives as we taste the resurrection life we testify about and live holistic lives marked by faith, hope, and love.

BENEDICTION: THE JOY OF JESUS

> *Joy, which was the small publicity of the pagan, is the gigantic secret of the Christian. . . . There was some one thing that was too great for God to show us when He walked upon our earth; and I have sometimes fancied that it was His mirth.*
>
> G. K. Chesterton, Orthodoxy

Though this is certainly a book about mission, at a more fundamental level this is a book about a person. In his letter to the Colossians, Paul described Jesus as "the image of the invisible God" (1:15)—a stunning assertion that suggests that if we want to know what God is like, we need look no further than the face of Jesus. Indeed, as Alan Hirsch has suggested, though it was certainly scandalous in a first-century context to suggest that Jesus was like God, perhaps the more shocking thing for us to consider in our twenty-first century context is the inverse.[1] Not only is Jesus like God; God is like Jesus.[2]

As such, it's striking to consider the ways the Gospels so consistently capture the manifold *humanity* of Jesus. At various points, he's described as hungry (Matthew 4:2) and thirsty (John 19:28), weary from his travels (John 4:6) and on the go (Luke 8:1). He's portrayed as having both a sharp intuition (Mark 2:8) and a soft heart (Luke 7:13). He cracks jokes (Matthew 7:3-5) and cooks breakfast (John 21:9); he goes to parties (Mark 2:15) and retreats to get some time alone (Luke 5:16). He celebrates holidays (Matthew 26:19), navigates family drama (Mark 3:31-35), and spends time with friends (Luke 8:1).

Similarly, the Gospels consistently describe Jesus as experiencing a myriad of emotions. The Jesus we meet in the Scriptures is overflowing with compassion (Matthew 14:14), brimming with conviction (Luke 9:51), angry at hubris (Mark 3:5), full of love (Mark 10:21), undone by grief (John 11:33-35), zealous against injustice (John 2:13-17), overwhelmed by sorrow (Mark 14:34), disturbed by suffering (Mark 1:41), and gentle in heart (Matthew 11:29).

Far from walking through the Galilean countryside in a state of divine detachment, the Jesus we encounter in the Gospels is gritty and authentic—he felt deeply, lived transparently, and loved generously. The Gospel writers don't hold back from describing him in all kinds of decidedly everyday ways that resonate with our own lives.

Perhaps our favorite picture of Jesus in the whole of the Gospels comes in Luke 10:17-24 (a portion of the narrative that follows right on the heels of one of the foundational texts for this entire book—the sending of the seventy-two in Luke 10:1-16, where we see the 4E genius of Jesus on full display). As we end this book, we want to return to this text again, but this time from a different angle. Not only because of what it reveals to us about Jesus' purposes, but also because of what it reveals to us about Jesus' person.

JESUS, FULL OF JOY

In these verses Luke offers an arrestingly unique description of Jesus: "Jesus, *full of joy* through the Holy Spirit" (Luke 10:21, emphasis ours). For all the ways he is characterized, nowhere else in the whole of the Gospel narratives is Jesus described as "full of joy." It's a singularly distinct description, and as such, it raises a question: What was it about this situation that made Jesus so joyful?

The setting described in Luke 10 was pulsing with the energy of possibility. What had begun as a mission filled with foreboding uncertainty—"I'm sending you out like lambs among wolves" (v. 3)—and marked by profound vulnerability—"Do not take a purse or bag or sandals" (v. 4)—had become a reunion of rejoicing. Surrounded by the teeming crowds they'd ministered to, thirty-six pairs of disciples returned to Jesus not with trepidation but jubilation: "The seventy-two returned with joy and said, 'Lord, even the demons submit to us in your name'" (v. 17).

It's not hard to imagine the amazed expressions on the disciples' faces as they recounted to one another (and to Jesus) the ways people welcomed them into their homes and responded to their teaching. Not only did they (somehow) preach with authority, they (inexplicably) saw people healed of illness, and (astonishingly) even the demons obeyed their commands to "be gone"!

What began as a simple directive to pray for God to send more workers into the harvest (v. 2) had become a bona fide revival that had now transformed dozens of communities across the countryside of Palestine through the manifest kingdom of God. The disciples had been successful beyond their wildest dreams and the impact of their work was swarming all around them—lives restored, salvation embraced, and deliverance demonstrated. The kingdom of God had broken out in power not just around but somehow *through* them, and we can imagine their excitement swelling as the leaders of a burgeoning missional movement. Surely *this* was the revival their people had been anticipating for generations, and against all odds, they were somehow in the middle of it.

It's in this environment that we witness Jesus "full of joy through the Holy Spirit." Not in the temple, surrounded by religious professionals performing their sacred duties, but in the open countryside, surrounded by anonymous amateurs having just taken their first steps of faith and now experiencing the fruit of their labor.

Indeed, it's this precise contrast that marks Jesus' declaration of praise to his Father in verse 21—"I praise you, Father, Lord of heaven and earth, because you have hidden these things from the wise and learned, and revealed them to little children. Yes, Father, for this is what you were pleased to do." Apparently, this choice to invert the way of the world by revealing the kingdom to "little children" was central to the pleasure of the Father, the praise of the Son, and the presence of the Holy Spirit.

As such, it's not an exaggeration to suggest that more than anything else in his earthly life—more than his disciples choosing to follow him, more than being used by God to perform powerful miracles, more than revealing the truths of the kingdom through his parables—it was the all-play empowerment of ordinary, everyday people to proclaim and demonstrate the kingdom of God that made Jesus uniquely joyful.

Think about that reality for a moment.

Though we know from other passages that Jesus certainly lived a life of joy, it's fascinating to consider that nothing made Jesus more demonstrably joyful than the expansion of the kingdom through the simple obedience of everyday people. It was ordinary folks—amateurs whose identities are lost to history but whose names are written in the book of life—offering their faithful yes to Jesus that filled him with the joy of the Holy Spirit and made his heart sing.

ENCOUNTERING JOY

When we consider "mission" it's easy to think about zeal, boldness, and risk, but it's our conviction that the reviving mission of Jesus is inextricably linked to joy.

We hope you've heard this kind of joy dripping from every story we've told about God's everyday movement through ordinary people. We hope you've heard it in the story of God bringing renewal to campuses through Naomi, God encountering Linson while he paged through his father's Bible in his dorm room, Megan's story of redemption with Native students, God bringing dignity through Carmen's call center, Alexis and Lindsay confronting the powers of death in Miami, and a church plant born through a *kairos* moment in a coffee shop.

We believe that the new season Jesus is releasing in our day will be marked by joy. Our conviction is that it is in fact Jesus' joy expressed through the lives of his followers around the world that might—perhaps more than anything else—subvert the pervasive anxiety of our cultural moment and mark a new way forward for the people of God.

The kind of reviving mission we've been describing is full of immense potential to accomplish the purposes of God. When we encounter God's with-us-and-on-the-move presence; explore our environments and relationships for his past, present, and future activity; empower the people God sends us through the Spirit he gives without measure; and establish rhythms of community to sustain life, the kingdom of God moves forward in dramatic ways.

Whether through the foundational ministry of Jesus and his disciples, the transformative rise of the early church, or the dramatic stories of impact we've sought to capture in this book, we believe the 4*E*s provide a framework for reviving mission in the way of Jesus. We've seen the ways this framework enables us as his followers to live lives of holistic mission marked by the presence of God, embodying the fruit of the Spirit, and overflowing with impact among our communities.

But.

As good as it is to live lives of impact, the best part of reviving mission in the way of Jesus isn't experiencing a life of purpose—it's encountering a person.

Though the language of Jesus' declaration in Luke 10:21 is a bit nondescript—"these things" are hidden/revealed and "all things" are committed to Jesus by his Father—as the passage continues, we see more clearly that these "things" aren't merely missiological principles. The fundamental object of revelation is the person of God in the face of Jesus—"no one knows who the Father is except the Son and those to whom the Son chooses to reveal him" (v. 22), and it's the climax of the passage that brings this idea into full relief.

Though the story starts with a broad, expansive frame—the seventy-two disciples (and those impacted by their ministry) returning to Jesus—as it continues, the focus narrows two different times.

First, it narrows to Jesus, full of joy through the Holy Spirit, declaring his praise to God in the midst of the crowd (vv. 21-22), and then a second time when Luke says, "He turned to his disciples and said privately . . . " (v. 23).

It's in the midst of the energy and expectation of the crowds teeming around them that Jesus offers this personal, private word to his disciples: "Blessed are the eyes that see what you see. For I tell you that many prophets and kings wanted to see what you see but did not see it, and to hear what you hear, but did not hear it" (vv. 23-24).

No doubt the disciples were seeing and hearing a lot in that moment. As they looked around they could see people who'd been healed by the power of God through their touch, transformed by the truth of God articulated in their preaching, and delivered from darkness by the authority of God in their words.

Further, we can imagine them looking around the circle at one another and being amazed at who they were becoming as they walked in the way of Jesus. Whether from years spent together on a fishing boat or months spent together following Jesus around the Galilean countryside, this community was no doubt painfully aware of each other's shortcomings and idiosyncrasies. Yet here they were—ordinary people being empowered by Jesus to proclaim and demonstrate the inbreaking of the kingdom of God!

As such, when Jesus speaks of prophets and kings wanting "to see what you see," we have to imagine that most certainly included the manifold movement of God all around them. In many ways they were watching the generational promises of God spoken to prophets like Moses, Isaiah, and Joel being fulfilled in real time in their midst.

And yet, we believe the burgeoning movement swelling around them was more secondary than primary—more background than foreground.

In the most immediate sense, what they were seeing and hearing when Jesus spoke to them wasn't the momentum or the crowds or even the cohesive affection of their community. What they saw when Jesus said, "Blessed are the eyes that see what you see," quite simply, was the joyful face of Jesus—the image of the invisible God smiling back at them.

A BLESSING OF JOY

As we end this book, it's *this* reality—the joyful smile of Jesus over your life—that we long for you to know most deeply.

To be sure, there is something undeniably beautiful about the whole people of God empowered for the whole mission of God. We cannot wait to hear about all the beautiful things God will do as you embrace his reviving mission. But we must remember that the greatest prize of following Jesus into mission isn't impact, fruit, or influence. The greatest reward of following Jesus is, quite simply, *Jesus*—encountering him, knowing his presence and pleasure, understanding that our lives brought him joy and made him smile. He is the one whom prophets and kings longed to see, and it's his joyful face that is the treasure hidden in the field and the pearl of great price.

Indeed, it's beholding the face of Jesus that is the end of our story: "The throne of God and of the Lamb will be in the city, and his servants will serve him. They will see his face, and his name will be on their foreheads" (Revelation 22:3-4). The good news of the gospel is that this isn't just a "someday" reality—it can be an everyday experience as we take our place in the great story of God and live lives of reviving mission that make Jesus glad.

So, as we continue to navigate the new season God is releasing in our midst, we wanted to end this book with a blessing.

May you know the freedom of being an amateur ambassador—a sent one dearly loved and fully empowered to embody the new normal of the kingdom of God that is at hand.

May you live a life infused with wonder as you encounter the ever-present and ever-moving person of God.

May you be marked by buoyant curiosity as you explore the past, present, and future work of the one who was and is and is to come.

May you give as generously as you've received, empowering others fully and without measure through the person of the Spirit.

May you know resilience as you establish habits and habitats to help life flourish wherever God sends you.

And at the end of all things, may your life be saturated with the affection of the joyful face of Jesus smiling at you every step of the way.

Epilogue

HERALDS OF A NEW NORMAL

It was a clear, crisp December day in Nebraska. We were together, spending time in prayer to recommit ourselves and this book to Jesus. As we were preparing to close the time of prayer and return to our writing, Eric said, "Hey, I think I maybe just heard something from Jesus."

He proceeded to share that he'd had the verse Habakkuk 2:3 come to his mind. As that's a relatively obscure Old Testament verse, we had no idea what it said. However, as God often speaks to Eric through those kinds of Bible "addresses," we looked the verse up, and we were stunned by what we read.

> Write down the revelation
>   and make it plain on tablets
>   so that a herald may run with it.
> For the revelation awaits an appointed time;
>   it speaks of the end
>   and will not prove false.
> Though it linger, wait for it;
>   it will certainly come
>   and will not delay. (Habakkuk 2:2-3)

As the words hung in the air, a holy hush fell over the room as we sat with the potential implications of that Scripture for this project. What might it mean to make these ideas as plain as possible? What should we make of the command to wait? How should we be encouraged by the certainty of the revelation coming to pass? Who were the heralds we were supposed to entrust these "tablets" to?

It's been said that revival is "a season of breakthroughs, in word, deed, and power, that lead to a new normal of kingdom experience and fruitfulness."[1] By faith we believe we are entering just such a "new normal" season when God pours out revival in history-shaping kinds of ways.

New seasons call for new expressions of faith—"new wineskins" of mission and community, and we are increasingly compelled by the ways the 4*E*s might become just such a "new wineskin" that God uses to renew his church, revive our mission, and revitalize our culture through lives of embodied gospel witness.

New seasons also call for new generations of leaders, and we believe God is raising up a new generation of global "heralds" who are ready to receive a fresh word from God and run with it. Ordinary women and men from all walks of life who are eager for a new way forward. Amateurs who are willing to yield their lives to the everyday movement of God. Heralds who are ready to embrace the reviving mission of Jesus in their neighborhoods, on their campuses, and in their communities.

Our conviction is that if you've made it this far, it's likely that *you* are one of these heralds and God is inviting you to take your place in the new season he is stirring all around us. As such, our prayer is that this book might be like a "second wind" in your lungs as you pursue the calling God has put on your life. We hope the ideas we've sought to "make plain" here might help you find your stride and stoke your resolve to follow Jesus wholeheartedly into his reviving mission.

In his letter to the Romans, Paul says that the whole of creation is groaning and waiting "in eager expectation for the children of God to be revealed" (Romans 8:19)—children who are heralds of a new season. Heralds who are not only aware of the problems around them but awakened to the dawn emerging on the horizon. Heralds who don't have it all figured out but who are ready to run into the new normal of Jesus' reviving mission. So, will you run with us?

ACKNOWLEDGMENTS

FROM ALL OF US: Of course, there are countless folks who have invested in this book that we want to thank! We're grateful for the team at IVP—especially our editors Al Hsu and Lisa Renninger, who have made this book better through their investment. Special thanks to our many pre-readers who offered such helpful, candid, and encouraging feedback—our wives Betina, Steph, and Stacy, who were often our pre-pre-readers (!), and many friends like Andrew, Camille, Clayton, HC, James, Jason, Kale, Kathy, Karen, Louan, Marty, Adam, Megan, Paul, Shawn, Serene, Sherami, Tammy, Tim C., and Tim L., who reviewed early drafts of our manuscript. We are grateful for you all!

We want to specifically acknowledge Shawn Young, InterVarsity's national director of chapter planting. A decade ago, Shawn commissioned Jon and Eric to develop a less staff-focused model for planting new ministries. It was that model that became the 4*E*s. Shawn, thank you for stewarding InterVarsity's apostolic calling and for making room for apostolic leaders to thrive!

From Linson:

I am grateful for my community at METRO Church for covering me in prayer and giving me space to write—as a church, we embody so many of the principles in this book. I am incredibly indebted to my training and education at Fuller Seminary, specifically the Asian American Center. Also, I would like to thank the South Asian InterVarsity community for giving me space to experiment and clarify many of the key lessons found throughout the book. I want to acknowledge my parents, in-laws, and siblings who have encouraged me to keep writing and leading despite challenges. Finally, thank you to Betina, Sophia, and JT for reminding me that life is much more than ministry, writing, teaching, and leading . . . thank you, and I love you!

From Jon:

I'm grateful for the countless people who have encouraged me along the way—more than I could possibly name here! Thank you, Mom and Dad, for laying a foundation of faith in our family. Thank you to the many mentors who have formed my life in manifold ways—particularly Andrew, Jason B., Tom, and Jason T. I'm grateful for many who have encouraged me in writing, especially professors Terence Kleven, Thomas Kopacek, and Rick Richardson; my pastor Kevin Korver; and friends like James and Beau. My heart is full of affection for the InterVarsity community, and I'm especially grateful to have been a part of the Central Region, the Underserved Geographies Cohort, and the Central US RD Team. Finally, I want to thank my family—Stephanie, Elijah, and Abigail—who have walked every step of this journey with me. I love you fam!

From Eric:

I'm grateful for InterVarsity's planting team: Shawn Young, Serene Neddenriep, Hans Franzen, Abner Ramos, and Phil Nordquist. Being in the laboratory of mission, prayer, and empowerment with you all has been a profound joy. I'm grateful for Pastor Jamison Horton and the One Hope Family, who have invested in me and made room for me to lead. Thank you to Salome Chuang and Elizabeth English for teaching me the way of Jesus. I'm grateful for the many students from UNO, UNL, and UNK who taught me so much about mission. Thanks Bill and Ann Hall for being family on mission with Stacy and me. Thank you, Mom and Dad, for making my life and calling possible. Memo, Lena, and Jonny, I'm grateful for the ways God has used you in my life to teach me what it means to be a dad first. Stacy, thank you for partnering with me in life and ministry for the last twenty years, and thank you for being my Abigail. Cuando olvido quién soy como hijo de Dios, tú me acuerdas.

NOTES

PREFACE: SIGNS OF A NEW SEASON

[1] Jon had the privilege of hearing this report firsthand from Brady Casper the morning after the outpouring broke out at Asbury.

1. A NEW SEASON AND A NEW WAY

[1] Talia Wise, "2023: A Year of Revival on College Campuses," God Reports, December 14, 2023, www.godreports.com/2023/12/2023-a-year-of-revival-on-college-campuses; and Abigail Reed, "Revival for a New Generation," Azusa Pacific University, August 3, 2023, www.apu.edu/articles/revival-for-a-new-generation.

[2] Victoria Pires, "How Hundreds of FSU Students Got Baptized in the Westcott Fountain," Her Campus, February 26, 2024, www.hercampus.com/school/fsu/campus-unite-fsu-how-hundreds-of-students-got-baptized-in-the-wescott-fountain.

[3] See "YLGen," Lausanne Movement, accessed March 23, 2024, https://lausanne.org/ylgen.

[4] Nana Yaw Offei Awuku, interview by Jon Hietbrink, March 22, 2024.

[5] I first heard about this story from Pete Grieg, "Something wonderful seems to be stirring," Facebook, May 7, 2024, www.facebook.com/pete.greig.1/posts/pfbid0364FchXMR7z6nY7DBA1Usv3UZDH27wHpKafrRwkiRzRAUhefsGAHhFbJ1CynhmPsol. I was able to confirm it via a firsthand account from my friend Sherami Hinders, who was in attendance at the event and provided this quote during an interview on May 8, 2024.

[6] Jim Memory, *Europe 2021: A Missiological Report*, European Christian Mission, www.ecmi.org/en/europe-2021-a-missiological-report.

[7] Caroline De Sury, "Record 12,000 People Were Baptized in France on Easter," *America*, April 4, 2024, www.americamagazine.org/faith/2024/04/04/france-easter-adult-baptism-record-247629.

[8] Jon had the privilege of hearing about this story from Ragnhild Steinsland, coordinator for Revive Communities. See www.reviveeurope.org.

[9] See "The Story," The Send, accessed July 23, 2024, https://thesend.org/story/.

10 Dwight and Mary Kay Martin, "Baptizing 1,588 Believers in Thailand," The Alliance, July 28, 2022, https://cmalliance.org/baptizing-1588-believers-in-thailand.

11 Abraham Bakari, "Over 10,000 Baptized in Eastern Nigeria at Baptism Festival," Adventist News Network, February 3, 2023, https://adventist.news/news/over-10-000-baptized-in-eastern-nigeria-at-baptism-festival.

12 Alex Murashko, "Mass Baptism in Southern California Described in 'Biblical Proportions,'" *Washington Times*, July 10, 2023, www.washingtontimes.com/news/2023/jul/10/mass-baptism-southern-california-described-biblica/.

13 Memory, *Europe 2021*.

14 Harvey Kwiyani, "Blessed Reflex: African Christians in Europe," *Missio Africanus* 3, no. 1 (2017): 40-49, https://missioafricanus.com/wp-content/uploads/2019/05/Harvey_Kwiyani_Blessed-Reflex-African-Christians-in-Europe.pdf.

15 Jim Memory, "The Extraordinary Re-evangelization of Europe," Lausanne Movement, October 14, 2021, https://lausanne.org/about/blog/the-extraordinary-re-evangelization-of-europe.

16 Uchenna D. Anyanwu, Cristian Castro, and David Ro, "Majority World Mission Movements," Lausanne Movement, https://lausanne.org/report/polycentric-christianity/majority-world-mission-movements.

17 "Disciple Making Movements," Lausanne Movement, https://lausanne.org/report/disciple-making-movements.

18 David Hoffman, "Even Bigger Than Asbury: A Powerful Move of God of 'Biblical Proportions' Is Unfolding Right Now," CBN, September 4, 2024, www2.cbn.com/news/world/even-bigger-asbury-powerful-move-god-biblical-proportions-unfolding-right-now.

19 Ammar Maleki and Pooyan Tamimi Arab, *Iranians' Attitudes Toward Religion: A 2020 Survey Report* (Netherlands: GAMAAN, 2020), https://gamaan.org/wp-content/uploads/2020/09/GAMAAN-Iran-Religion-Survey-2020-English.pdf.

20 At least some of this growth is being fueled by the Pars Theological Center (see https://parstheology.org), where five hundred students are currently enrolled in theological studies even as they serve the church.

21 Pete Greig, Twitter/X, February 14, 2023, https://twitter.com/PeteGreig/status/1625498379236311043.

22 In addition to the more grassroots stories we've captured in this chapter, it's worth noting that the last several years have also seen the emergence of a new wave of organizational collaboration and an acceleration of ministries contending for global revival and mission. We're particularly grateful for movements like Pulse/

Together (https://pulse.org), THE SEND (https://thesend.org), and Unite Us (www.uniteusmovement.com), which have hosted stadium-sized events filled with believers seeking God and being commissioned into global witness. We're celebrating coalitions such as EveryTribe EveryNation (https://eten.bible) and EveryCampus (https://everycampus.com)—historic partnerships of interorganizational collaboration for the sake of jointly shared missional priorities. We're encouraged by church-planting movements like NewThing (https://newthing.org/), which is seeing a remarkable acceleration of their efforts around the world. We're inspired by networks like 24-7 Prayer (https://www.24-7prayer.com/) and Revive Europe Movement (www.reviveeurope.org/), which are stoking the collective longing for revival and contending for awakening across Europe and around the world.

[23] Author Andy Crouch aptly used an even more intense version of this metaphor when he suggested in March 2020 that Covid-19 would not be merely a "blizzard" or a "winter" but rather an "ice age" that would be remembered as a turning point of history. Indeed, it seems that he was unfortunately all too prescient as virtually every person on the planet has been affected by the turmoil of the last few years. See Andy Crouch, Kurt Keilhacker, and Dave Blanchard, "Leading Beyond the Blizzard: Why Every Organization Is Now a Startup," The Praxis Journal, March 20, 2020, https://journal.praxislabs.org/leading-beyond-the-blizzard-why-every-organization-is-now-a-startup-b7f32fb278ff.

[24] Mark Sayers, "From a Complicated World to a Complex World," *Rebuilders* podcast, July 14, 2021, https://rebuilders.co/podcasts/2021/7/14/rebuilders-from-a-complicated-world-to-a-complex-world.

[25] See Christianity Today, *The Rise and Fall of Mars Hill*, podcast, May 2021, www.christianitytoday.com/ct/podcasts/rise-and-fall-of-mars-hill/; *Shiny Happy People: Duggar Family Secrets*, directed by Julia Willoughby Nason and Olivia Crist, 2023, www.amazon.com/Shiny-Happy-People-Duggar-Secrets/dp/B0B8TR2QV5.

[26] A 2018 Barna survey found that rates of atheism among Gen Z were double that of previous generations ("Atheism Doubles Among Generation Z," Barna, January 24, 2018, www.barna.com/research/atheism-doubles-among-generation-z), and currently only 17 percent of US young adults age eighteen to twenty-two consider themselves committed Christians, which is roughly half the rate of thirteen- to eighteen-year-olds ("Over Half of Gen Z Teens Feel Motivated to Learn More About Jesus," Barna, February 1, 2023, www.barna.com/research/teens-and-jesus).

[27] "38% of U.S. Pastors Have Thought About Quitting Full-Time Ministry in the Past Year," Barna, November 16, 2021, https://www.barna.com/research/pastors-well-being.

28 Jamie Ducharme, "Feeling Off? It Could Be 'Ambient' Stress," *Time*, February 15, 2024, https://time.com/6201005/ambient-stress-pandemic-mental-health.

29 We're indebted to our brother Nana Yaw Offei Awuku, who shared this proverb with us during an interview for this book.

30 Alan Hirsch defines Christendom as "the standardized form and expression of the church and mission formed in the post-Constantine period." *The Forgotten Ways* (Grand Rapids, MI: Brazos, 2009), 276.

31 We borrowed this phrase from our friend Trent Sheppard, who has written a compelling book on the "ordinary" life of Jesus titled *Jesus Journey: Shattering the Stained Glass Superhero and Discovering the Humanity of God* (Grand Rapids, MI: Zondervan, 2017).

32 It's fascinating to consider how little we know about the backstories of most of the disciples Jesus called. Though we know the twelve included two pairs of fisherman brothers (Peter and Andrew, James and John), a tax collector named Levi, and a zealot named Simon, fully half of the twelve disciples—Philip, Bartholomew, Thomas, James, Thaddeus, and Judas—appear only as names completely devoid of backstory (Mark 3:16-19).

33 Jesus' parables are full of irony, ridiculous contrasts, and puns. One example can be found in Matthew 23:24, where Jesus makes an example of the Pharisees by saying, "You strain out a gnat but swallow a camel." Though it's easy to lose the humor in translation, the Aramaic reveals a pun, as the word for "gnat" was *galma*, while the word for "camel" was *gamla*. See Tim Schenck, "The Often Overlooked Humor of Jesus," *Clergy Family Confidential* blog, May 30, 2013, https://frtim.wordpress.com/2013/05/30/the-often-overlooked-humor-of-jesus.

34 Ray Konig, "What Happened to the Apostles?" About-Jesus.org, www.about-jesus.org/martyrs.htm, accessed April 14, 2024.

35 Indeed, whether through the persecution of Rome during the 30s through 60s or the destruction of the Jerusalem temple in 70 CE, each of the original disciples lived through a season of profound disruption.

36 Christianity was granted legal recognition by the Roman Empire in 313 CE, and by 380 CE it was declared the official religion of the Roman Empire.

37 Rodney Stark, *The Rise of Christianity* (Princeton, NJ: Princeton University Press, 1996), 214-15.

38 See the disciples' question in Mark 4:41—"Who is this?"—or the entire exchange captured in Luke 9:18-56.

39 For more on the rise of religious consumerism, see Hirsch, *Forgotten Ways*, 106-12.

40 This is the pattern we see in Mark 1:29, 1:32-34, and 2:1, where Jesus first ministers *in* Simon Peter's home to heal his mother-in-law, then ministers *from* that same

home to the entire town, and returns *to* that same home when he comes back to Capernaum.

⁴¹ Though Cornelius is not mentioned explicitly, we know from Acts 21 that the church in Caesarea grew to involve multiple households of disciples—including those of Philip (Acts 21:8) and Mnason (21:16)—who would welcome Paul on his journey to Jerusalem.

⁴² We have to imagine that Paul had Lydia and her network firmly in view when he says in Philippians, "I thank my God every time I remember you" (1:3).

2. JESUS' HOLISTIC MISSION

¹ You can learn more about this remarkable (and ongoing) global movement at https://www.24-7prayer.com or through Pete Greig and Dave Roberts's *Red Moon Rising* (Lake Mary, FL: Relevant Books, 2003).

² *Merriam-Webster*, s.v. "missiology," accessed May 21, 2024, www.merriam-webster.com/dictionary/missiology.

³ David Bosch, *Transforming Mission: Paradigm Shifts in Theology of Mission* (Maryknoll, NY: Orbis Books, 1991), 1.

⁴ In this space, we're indebted to Roger Martin, whose work on the "knowledge funnel" of mystery, heuristic, and algorithm roughly approximates this threefold model. See Martin's work in *The Design of Business* (Brighton, MA: Harvard Business Review Press, 2009) for more.

3. ENCOUNTER: GOD IS HERE

¹ Kandi Wiens, "Has Cynicism Infected Your Organization?" *Harvard Business Review*, May 25, 2023, https://hbr.org/2023/05/has-cynicism-infected-your-organization.

² Dacher Keltner, *Awe: The New Science of Everyday Wonder and How It Can Transform Your Life* (New York: Penguin Press, 2023), 34.

³ The Psalms are full of this kind of transformation; see Psalm 27, 42, or 63 for some particular examples.

⁴ See Mike Cosper, *Recapturing the Wonder: Transcendent Faith in a Disenchanted World* (Downers Grove, IL: InterVarsity Press, 2017).

⁵ Wayne Grudem, *Systematic Theology* (Grand Rapids, MI: Zondervan Academic, 1994), 267-71.

⁶ Grudem, *Systematic Theology*, 267-71.

⁷ Simon Sinek, *Start with Why* (New York: Penguin Group, 2009), 39.

⁸ Mark Sayers, *A Non-Anxious Presence: How a Changing and Complex World Will Create a Remnant of Renewed Christian Leaders* (Chicago: Moody Publishers, 2022), 31.

⁹ Michael S. Heiser, *The Unseen Realm: Recovering the Supernatural Worldview of the Bible* (Bellingham, WA: Lexham Press, 2015), 332-34.

¹⁰ Dallas Willard, *The Spirit of Disciplines: Understanding How God Changes Lives* (New York: HarperCollins, 1991), 210.

¹¹ We love the Lectio365 app from 24-7 Prayer, which includes a morning and evening audio devotional that uses this style of prayer. See https://www.24-7prayer.com/resource/lectio-365.

¹² Jon Tyson, "God Comes Where He's Wanted," Church of the City of New York, YouTube video, January 10, 2023, www.youtube.com/watch?v=8W9BQAjQN8s.

¹³ Dallas Willard, *The Great Omission* (San Francisco: HarperCollins, 2006), 37.

¹⁴ Mark Batterson, *The Circle Maker: Praying Circles Around Your Biggest Dreams and Greatest Fears* (Grand Rapids, MI: Zondervan, 2016), 215.

4. ENCOUNTER: GOD IS MOVING

¹ C. R. Golsworthy, "A Tribute to Bro. Bakht Singh: He Taught Us to Pray," Brother Bakht Singh, accessed April 20, 2024, www.brotherbakhtsingh.org/PDF%20files/Taught_to_Pray.pdf.

² Sam George, "*Motus Dei* (The Move of God): A Theology and Missiology for a Moving World," in *Asian Diaspora Christianity*, ed. Sam George, vol. 3, *Reflections of Asian Diaspora: Mapping Theologies and Ministries* (Minneapolis: Fortress, 2022), 95-122.

³ Prince Kumar Tamilarasan, "The Displaced and Divine Self-Exile: The Interplay between the Absence and Presence of God," in *Reflections of Asian Diaspora*, 49-68.

⁴ Darryl Wooldridge, "Drive for the Divine," *HTS Teologiese Studies/Theological Studies* 71, no. 3 (2015): 8, https://doi.org/10.4102/hts.v71i3.2997.

⁵ Dan Van Veen, "More Than a Dream: Muslims Coming to Christ," AG News, May 30, 2023, https://news.ag.org/en/article-repository/news/2023/05/more-than-a-dream-muslims-coming-to-christ.

⁶ Sister Vandana, *Waters of Fire: St John's Gospel in the Light of Vedanta*, 3rd ed. (Bangalore: ATC, 1989; first published, Madras: Christian Literature Society, 1981)

⁷ See Don Richardson, *Peace Child*, 4th ed. (Ventura, CA: Regal Books, 2005).

⁸ Justo L. Gonzales, *Santa Biblia: The Bible Through Hispanic Eyes* (Nashville, TN: Abingdon Press, 1996), 82-87

⁹ Paul picks up this idea before the Athenian Areopagus in Acts 17:26 when he says, "[God] marked out their appointed times in history and the boundaries of their lands."

¹⁰ Our dear friend Beau Crosetto has written a great book on this topic called *Beyond Awkward: When Talking about Jesus Is Outside Your Comfort Zone* (Downers Grove, IL: InterVarsity Press, 2014).

Notes to Pages 72-114

11 Thomas R. Kelly, in Thomas R. Kelly, Douglas V. Steere, and Richard J. Foster, *A Testament of Devotion* (San Francisco: HarperSanFrancisco, 1996), 33.

12 Jesus' instructions to his disciples in Mark 14:13-16 is another fascinating example of this pattern.

13 Sam George, "God on the Move," interview by Jerome Blanco, *Fuller Studio*, Wheaton College Billy Graham Center, November 27, 2023, https://wheatonbillygraham.com/god-on-the-move-with-sam-george.

5. EXPLORE: LIFT UP YOUR EYES

1 See Numbers 24:2-9; Joshua 5:13; 1 Chronicles 21:16; Zechariah 5:5.

2 See Genesis 13:14-15; Isaiah 60:4.

3 See Genesis 22:4; 33:1; 1 Samuel 6:13.

4 Ellie Lisitsa, "The Trouble with Contempt," Gottman Institute, accessed on March 23, 2024, www.gottman.com/blog/self-care-contempt.

5 Malcolm Gladwell, *Blink* (Harlow, UK: Penguin Books, 2006), 32.

6 G. E. Wright, *Shechem, the Biography of a Biblical City* (New York: McGraw-Hill, 1965).

7 Diogenes Laertius, *Lives of Eminent Philosophers* 10.109-15.

8 Don Richardson, *Eternity in Their Hearts* (Ventura, CA: Regal Books, 1984), 14.

9 In fact, Paul quoted another line from this exact same poem by Epimenides when he wrote his letter to Titus: "One of Crete's own prophets has said it: 'Cretans are always liars, evil brutes, lazy gluttons'" (Titus 1:12). Paul quoted Epimenides twice and even referred to him as a prophet! See J. Rendel Harris, "A Further Note on the Cretans," *The Expositor* 3, no. 7 (April 1907): 332-37, available via Internet Archive, https://archive.org/details/expositor190703coxs/page/336/mode/2up.

10 Paul's sermon in Athens even flows from past (God made the whole world; for a time he overlooked our ignorance) to present (God is not far from each one of us; now he commands all people to repent) to the future (God has fixed a day when he will judge the world in righteousness).

6. EXPLORE: PEOPLE OF PEACE

1 This is another example of God moving with his people, even through painful circumstances. Here Priscilla and Aquila and their household experience the diaspora and ecclesia pattern from chapter four.

2 For example, look how the chief priests and Pharisees responded to the miracle of Lazarus being raised from the dead (John 11:53; 12:10).

7. EMPOWER: BY WHAT POWER?

[1] Norman Grubb, *Touching the Invisible* (Fort Washington, PA: CLC Publications, 1940), 18.

[2] Richard Rohr, *Things Hidden: Scripture as Spirituality* (Cincinnati, OH: Franciscan Media, 2007), 74.

[3] Jordan Seng, *Miracle Work* (Downers Grove, IL: InterVarsity Press, 2012), 55.

[4] Seng, *Miracle Work*, 69.

[5] Seng, *Miracle Work*, 70.

[6] James Choung and Ryan Pfeiffer, *Longing for Revival: From Holy Discontent to Breakthrough Faith* (Downers Grove, IL: InterVarsity Press, 2020), 154-70.

8. EMPOWER: SERVE AND SEND

[1] Chuck DeGroat, *When Narcissism Comes to Church* (Downers Grove, IL: InterVarsity Press, 2020), 71.

9. ESTABLISH: GOD OF CADENCE

[1] James Clear, *Atomic Habits: An Easy and Proven Way to Build Good Habits and Break Bad Ones* (New York: Penguin, 2018), 15.

[2] Clear, *Atomic Habits*, 15-16.

[3] James Strong, *Strong's Exhaustive Concordance of the Bible* (Nashville, TN: Abingdon Press, 1890), Strongs #5550.

[4] Strong, *Strong's Exhaustive Concordance of the Bible*, Strongs #2540.

[5] Leonard Ravenhill has been attributed to this quote in many publications, but notably this quote was used to explain *kairos* during the Brownsville Revival by leaders John Kilpatrick, Steve Hill, and Lindell Cooley.

[6] James Clear, "How To Start New Habits That Actually Stick," James Clear website, accessed March 20, 2024, https://jamesclear.com/three-steps-habit-change.

[7] Alan Hirsch, *The Forgotten Ways* (Grand Rapids, MI: Brazos Press, 2006), 18.

[8] Alan Kreider, *The Patient Ferment of the Early Church: The Improbable Rise of Christianity in the Roman Empire* (Grand Rapids, MI: Baker Academic, 2016), 129.

[9] Rodney Stark, *The Rise of Christianity: A Sociologist Reconsiders History* (Princeton, NJ: Princeton University Press, 1996), 161.

10. ESTABLISH: GOD OF THE GARDEN-CITY

[1] Bruce K. Waltke, *Genesis: A Commentary* (New York: HarperCollins Christian Publishing, 2001), 85.

[2] Jürgen Moltmann, *The Trinity and the Kingdom: The Doctrine of God* (San Francisco: HarperSanFrancisco, 1991), ebook, loc. 1572.

³ Gordon D. Fee, *Revelation: A New Covenant Commentary* (Cambridge, UK: Lutterworth Press, 2013), 303.

⁴ James Strong, *Strong's Exhaustive Concordance of the Bible* (Nashville, TN: Abingdon Press, 1890), Strongs #G3624.

⁵ JR Woodward and Dan White Jr., *Church as Movement: Starting and Sustaining Missional-Incarnational Communities* (Downers Grove, IL: InterVarsity Press, 2016), 156.

⁶ Figure 10.1 adapted from Woodward and White, *Church as Movement*.

⁷ Brent Gleeson, "The Coronavirus Challenge: A Navy SEAL's Guide to Leading Through Adversity," Forbes, March 16, 2020, www.forbes.com/sites/brentgleeson/2020/03/16/the-coronavirus-challenge-a-navy-seals-guide-to-leading-through-adversity/.

⁸ Steven Johnson, *Where Good Ideas Come From: The Natural History of Innovation* (New York: Penguin Random House, 2010), 43-66.

⁹ Nassim Nicholas Taleb, *Antifragile: Things That Gain from Disorder* (New York: Random House, 2014), 3-4.

¹⁰ Woodward and White, *Church as Movement*, 160.

¹¹ Woodward and White, *Church as Movement*, 158.

¹² Neil Cole, *Organic Leadership: Leading Naturally Right Where You Are* (Grand Rapids, MI: Baker Books, 2009), 137.

¹³ Jim Collins, *BE 2.0 (Beyond Entrepreneurship 2.0): Turning Your Business into an Enduring Great Company* (New York: Penguin Random House, 2020), 165.

CONCLUSION: THE JOY OF JESUS

¹ Alan Hirsch, "The whole point of the Incarnation," Twitter/X, August 4, 2019, https://x.com/alanhirsch/status/1158038637453463552.

² See N. T. Wright's article "How Jesus Saw Himself," https://library.biblicalarchaeology.org/article/how-jesus-saw-himself.

EPILOGUE: HERALDS OF A NEW NORMAL

¹ James Choung and Ryan Pfeiffer, *Longing for Revival: From Holy Discontent to Breakthrough Faith* (Downers Grove, IL: InterVarsity Press, 2020), 17.

Want more resources to help your church or ministry awaken to the everyday movement of God?

www.revivingmission.org

Like this book?
Scan the code to discover more content like this!

Get on IVP's email list to receive special offers, exclusive book news, and thoughtful content from your favorite authors on topics you care about.

IVPRESS.COM/BOOK-QR